P9-ELP-324

Best American Short Plays Series

THE
BEST
AMERICAN
SHORT
PLAYS
1996-1997

Other Play Anthologies from Applause

ASIAN AMERICAN DRAMA: Nine Plays from the Multiethnic Landscape edited by Brian Nelson

BLACK COMEDY: a Critical Anthology of Nine Plays, Interviews, and Essays edited by Pamela Faith Jackson

THE NATIONAL BLACK DRAMA ANTHOLOGY: Eleven Plays from America's Leading African American Theaters edited by Woodie King, Jr.

HERE TO STAY: Five Plays from the Women's Project edited by Julia Miles

PLAYS BY AMERICAN WOMEN 1900-1930 edited by Judith Barlow

PLAYS BY AMERICAN WOMEN 1930-1960 edited by Judith Barlow

WOMEN ON THE VERGE: Seven Avant-Garde American Plays edited by Rosette C. Lamont

AMAZON ALL-STARS: Thirteen Lesbian Plays edited by Rosemary Keefe Curb

A FLEA IN HER REAR (OR ANTS IN HER PANTS) and Nine Other Vintage French Farces

THEATRE FOR YOUNG AUDIENCES: Around the World in Twenty-One Plays edited by Lowell Swortzell

Best American Short Plays Series

THE
BEST
AMERICAN
SHORT
PLAYS
1996-1997

edited by
GLENN YOUNG

APPLAUSE
NEW YORK • LONDON

PJC MIL CAMPUS LRC

AN APPLAUSE ORIGINAL

THE BEST AMERICAN SHORT PLAYS 1996-1997

No part of this publication may be reproduced or transmitted in any form or by any means, electronic or mechanical, including photocopy, recording, or any information storage or retrieval system now known to be invented, without permission in writing from the publishers, except by a reviewer who wishes to quote brief passages in connection with a review written for inclusion in a magazine, newspaper or broadcast.

NOTE: All plays contained in this volume are fully protected under the Copyright Laws of the United States of America, the British Empire, including the Dominion of Canada, and all other countries of the International Copyright Union and the Universal Copyright Convention. Permission to reproduce, wholly or in part, by any method, must be obtained from the copyright owners or their agents. (See CAUTION notices at the beginning of each play.)

Copyright ©1998 by Applause Theatre Book Publishers
All Rights Reserved
ISBN 1-55783-316-8 (cloth), 1-55783-317-6 (paper)
ISSN 0067-6284

Applause Theatre Book Publishers
211 West 71st Street
New York, NY 10023
Phone: (212) 595-4735
Fax: (212) 721-2856

A & C Black
Howard Road, Eaton Socon
Huntingdon, Cambs PC19 3CZ
Phone: 01480-212666
Fax: 01480-405014

First Applause Printing, 1998

CONTENTS

To Howard and Marianne Stein

INTRODUCTION

"Mr. Albee," one of Edward Albee's early admirers once accosted him after a performance of *Sandbox*, "I love your work so much. I simply cannot wait until you write a full-length play." "Madam," Mr. Albee responded, "there's no need for you to wait any longer. You'll find that all my plays are full-length."

Albee's reply might be the motto of this series. The short play is not short on anything. It's as full as the longest play by Lope de Vega. The short play isn't missing anything either — it wouldn't know where to put a second act. Short plays need more length the way sonnets need a fifteenth line. A short play may be briefer than a "full-length" play, but is no less complete.

Sandbox debuted in print in the 1960 edition of this annual, under the editorship of Margaret Mayorga. Since Ms. Mayorga's remarkable tenure other editors — including Stanley Richards, Ramon Delgado, Howard Stein, and myself — have endeavored to keep her standard flying equally high. In this volume, then, as in the sixty preceding volumes of the series, a dozen "full-length" plays await your fullest attention.

The following is a short, cordial introduction to each of this year's dazzling dozen:

The student in Neena Beber's *Misreadings* balks at the syllabus and thumbs her nose at the final exam, but both student and professor earn a grade of woefully incomplete by play's end. Each is called to account by the other in a way that invokes — yet leans ironically on — Aristotle's maxim of "the unexamined life."

In *The Rehearsal, A Fantasy* J. Rufus Caleb strums up vibrant, echoing shadows of Jimi Hendrix and Little Richard in a marathon dual jam session of Oedipal proportions. As they play back the tape of their previous night's concert, both rockers also rewind through the drama of their lives together. Young Jimi, no longer content simply to support his mentor's music, looks longingly for an exit to the beginning of his own sound. The pain and ambivalence of their onrushing split turns the volume and tone up louder and shriller, producing a verbal music both mournful and electric.

The machines have the orgasms in Edward de Grazia's "opera," *The Vacuum Cleaner*, while human beings sputter and peter out — pun intended. The spring in de Grazia's characters' steps is not related to love in the air. The lyrics they sing are robotic platitudes, decrepit vestiges of a long lost language of a nearly extinct race. Lifetime warranties, it turns out, only apply to mechanical psyches nowadays.

Information and data petulantly refuse to be tamed into knowledge and wisdom in Christopher Durang's *Mrs. Sorken*. The title character, in her best Ladies' Club style, wishes to share with us her intelligent observations about The Theatre. (She enthuses somewhat in the style of Chekhov's lecturer in *The Harmfulness of Tobacco)* What issues forth, however, is a tangled torrent of dreamlike malapropisms, the underlying subject of which is our current pathetic degeneration from the heights of true classical theatre tradition.

Gus Edwards' subject, in his play *Four Walls*, is the easy fraudulence of life. Fakes of all brands and species are a lot easier to come by than the genuine article. But, with time, what's false may prove as dangerously seductive as the real thing. The cheap facsimile of life that Edwards' characters assemble becomes a shrine to which they not only offer worship but are sacrificed.

In Herb Gardner's *I'm With Ya, Duke*, Sam may be in utter misery at being ignored by history, but he takes surprising pleasure in his lament. His complaints about his son, "Dopey," and his larcenous business partner, Shimkin, are rich comic arias of blissful discontent. Sam may even forfeit his last chance for a life-saving operation because he's too busy taking a swipe at every suspect enemy. It takes a WASP doctor to set Sam straight about who's responsible for his fate. In facing the answer to the doctor's challenge, Sam finally faces his most challenging enemy, himself.

The patter of familiar domesticity in Susan Hansell's *My Medea* exudes a force much deeper than any from our own experience. Hansell's play, with its hip choral voiceover that makes it rap, is not merely a 90's L.A. cosmetic makeover of the Medea myth. Hansell also exercises her plot with originality and vigor. Nor is her gilded, hyperbolic invocation of O.J. Simpson & Co. throughout the play merely the rhetoric of clever political parody. Hansell's MEDEA cries out for blood with the authority and judgment of hard-core tragedy.

An emotionally challenged brother (a.k.a. the typical macho sports-car-driving yuppie) meets his physically challenged younger sibling in Rich Orloff's *I Didn't Know You Could Cook*. They finally network a dinner together amidst Mark's planes and other upwardly mobile appointments. Jerome is a stripped down version of his older brother: paraplegic, a teacher in an urban public school, gay; he has a specially adapted basic Ford in the garage. But Jerome isn't serving any empty calories tonight. He's dishing up a stiff brew of reality to wake his brother up to the relationship they've been miss-scheduling for a lifetime.

"I'm keeping very busy with external activities so I don't have to experience any inner feelings," explains Gary in *The Tunnel of Love*. In Jacquelyn Reingold's universe, professional inspectors (shrinks, physicians, analysts, and other experts) have effectively closed down not only Gary's but everyone's most basic instincts of creativity and introspection. The high-priced Peeping Toms with diplomas in *The Tunnel of Love* even replace our congenital reflexes with their committees on feelings. Reingold's tunnel might at first seem a one-way express lane for female metaphor, but the traffic backed up in this underground passage includes us all.

A contemporary master of the short play, Murray Schisgal can sock more power and complexity into a few pages than the earnest long-fellows can sandwich into a triptych of evenings. The audacious whimsy of Schisgal's writing teases then sweeps us into a gyration of collapsing time and place. His characters are ever eloquent, yet their brief conversation across the page rivals a haiku for economy. His *Fifty Years Ago* is no exception. What begins ostensibly as a first wedding anniversary tête-à-tête eventually invokes, involves, and invites the greatest celebrities of the Second World War. And while the couple's anniversary also celebrates the breaking out of peace on VJ Day, we are not permitted to forget that peace on all fronts, domestic and otherwise, is a temporary "occasion" performed in front of a backdrop of violence and war.

Lance in Lanford Wilson's *Your Everyday Ghost Story* tiptoes around the periphery of life, negotiating past unpleasantness with his famous charm and wit. He deflects dangerous realities as skillfully as he avoids a dying friend on the street. As his gay friends suffer and evanesce physically, however, Lance himself becomes increasingly insubstantial spiritually. The ghosts in Wilson's story are not the deceased but those survivors who keep themselves a dimension removed, forever superficial and forever without the solidity of real compassion.

Past the paparazzi, past the police blockades, a real estate agent escorts her prospect into the house that is the notorious scene of a recent crime in *Wildwood Park*, Seller and buyer traverse Doug Wright's ominous blank stage and, of course, we the audience follow them, urging the grand tour on to scenes of ever more grisly horror. "I'm a monster!" chirps the well-heeled agent. As we are drawn deeper into the dark web of speculation, we catch a glimpse and a whiff of the victims and the perpetrators, but we never learn any hard and fast details of the crime. And Wright never actually tells us what happened. Our final speculation must be that the crime is in the heart of the beholder and that the property offered for sale can only be purchased — however dearly — by the imagination.

— GLENN YOUNG

December, 1997

Neena Beber

MISREADINGS

Misreadings by Neena Beber. Copyright © 1997 by Neena Beber. All rights reserved. Reprinted by permission of Samuel French.

CAUTION: Professionals and amateurs are hereby warned that *Misreadings* by Neena Beber is subject to a royalty. It is fully protected under the copyright laws of the United States of America, and of all countries covered by the International Copyright Union (including the Dominion of Canada and the rest of the British Commonwealth), and of all countries covered by the Pan-American Convention and the Universal Copyright Convention, and of all countries with which the United States has reciprocal copyright relations. All rights, including professional, amateur, motion picture, recitation, lecturing, public reading, radio broadcasting, television, video or sound taping, all other forms of mechanical or electronic reproduction, such as information storage and retrieval systems and photocopying, and the rights of translation into foreign languages, are strictly reserved. Particular emphasis is placed upon the question of readings, permission for which must be secured from the author's agent in writing.

All inquiries should be addressed to Samuel French, 45 W. 25th Street, New York, NY 10010.

Neena Beber

Neena Beber's plays include *A Common Vision, Tomorrowland, The Brief but Exemplary Life of the Living Goddess, Failure to Thrive,* and *The Course of It.* Theatres that have produced her work include The Magic Theatre, New Georges, Watermark, circus minimus, Workhouse Theatre, Padua Hills Playwrights Festival, and En Garde Arts. Her plays have been workshopped and developed at The Playwrights Center's Midwest Playlabs, Audrey Skirball-Kenis Theatre, New York Theatre Workshop, The Public Theatre's New Works Project, Circle Rep Lab, South Coast Rep, MCC, GeVa Theatre, and Lincoln Center's Directors' Lab, among other places. Her short film, *Bad Dates,* was based on her one-act *Food.* Beber has received commissions from Amblin Entertainment/Playwrights Horizons and Sundance Children's Theatre, and a MacDowell Colony Fellowship. She has contributed articles to *American Theatre, Theatre,* and, *Performing Arts Journal.* Her writing for children's television has garnered Emmy and Ace Award nominations. She graduated *magna cum laude* from Harvard, specializing in Latin American Literature, and received her M.F.A. from N.Y.U.'s Dramatic Writing Program, where she was a Paulette Goddard Fellow. Beber grew up in Miami, Florida.

Misreadings was commissioned by Actors Theatre of Louisville and included in the 21st annual Humana Festival of New American Plays.

CHARACTERS

SIMONE   a student

RUTH   a teacher

A college professor's office, minimally represented: a desk with a very tall stack of blue exam composition books on it.

[*Lights up on* SIMONE.]

SIMONE: It's important to dress right. I want to look slick. To look sleek. To look like a fresh thing. I've got a message. I'm the message. Study me, baby, because in ten minutes, I'll be outta here.

[SIMONE *lights a cigarette. Lights up on* RUTH.]

RUTH: What are the issues for which you would kill?

    I like to ask my students this on their first day of class. I assign novels where the hero or heroine kills, or is killed. I try to bring it home.

    They tell me they would kill to defend their family. They'd kill to defend their friends. I ask them if they would kill for their country . . . for their freedom . . . what would it take?

SIMONE: I'd kill for a pair of Prada velvet platforms in deep plum. Those are to die for.

RUTH: Simone. I didn't know what she was doing in my class. Neither did she, apparently.

    [*To* SIMONE.] Nice segue, Simone; would we be willing to die for the same things we'd kill for?

    [*Out.*] She usually sat in the back, rarely spoke, wore too much lipstick and some costume straight out of, what, Vogue. When she did speak, it was always — disruptive.

SIMONE: I'd die for love except there ain't no Romeos, not that I've seen; I'd take a bullet for my daddy but he's already dead; I'd die of boredom if it were lethal, but I guess it isn't.

RUTH: If I couldn't inspire her, I wanted her gone. I'd asked her to come to my office hours. I asked her several times. She was failing, obviously. I would have let her drop the class, but it was too

RUTH: [*Cont'd.*] late for that. She never bothered to come see me. Not until the day before the final exam. She wanted me to give her a passing grade.

[RUTH *turns to* SIMONE.]

RUTH: How can I do that, Simone? You haven't even read the material. Have you read any of the material?

SIMONE: I don't find it relevant.

RUTH: If you haven't read it, how do you know?

SIMONE: I read the back covers.

RUTH: You may find yourself surprised... *Anna Karenina* is wonderful.

SIMONE: It's long.

RUTH: Why not give it a shot?

SIMONE: The books you assign are depressing... I don't want to be depressed. Why read stuff that brings you down? Kafka, Jesus Christ — I started it, okay? The guy was fucked up.

RUTH: So you were moved at least.

SIMONE: Moved to shut the book and find something more interesting to do.

RUTH: That's too bad; you might have found one of these books getting under your skin, if you stuck with it. Haven't you ever read something that's really moved you?

SIMONE: Nothing moves me, Dr. Ruth.

RUTH: I'm going to have to ask you to put out that cigarette.

SIMONE: Okay, ask. [*But she puts it out.*] See art or be art. I choose the latter.

RUTH: Somebody must be paying for this education of yours. I imagine they expect a certain return for their money.

SIMONE: How do you know I'm not the one paying for it?

RUTH: I don't believe someone who was spending their own money would waste it so flagrantly.

SIMONE: Okay, Dad chips in.

RUTH: Would that be the same father you said was dead?

SIMONE: That was a joke or a lie, take your pick.

RUTH: You're frustrating the hell out of me, Simone.

SIMONE: I don't consider it a waste, you know. I like the socialization part.

RUTH: If you fail out of this school, you won't be doing any more "socialization."

SIMONE: You assume that I'm failing the others.

RUTH: So it's just this class, then? That you have a problem with?

SIMONE: [Referring to her grammar.] Dangling. [Beat.] Do you enjoy being a teacher?

RUTH: Yes, I do.

SIMONE: So I'm paying for your enjoyment.

RUTH: It's not a sin to enjoy one's work, Simone.

SIMONE: I just don't think you should charge me, if it's more for your pleasure than for mine.

RUTH: I didn't say that.

SIMONE: Did you ever want to teach at a real school, not some second-rate institution like this?

RUTH: I like my job. You're not going to convince me otherwise.

SIMONE: Four-thousand two-hundred and ninety-eight.

RUTH: That is—?

SIMONE: Dollars. That's a lot of money. Do you think you're worth it? Do you think this class is worth it? Because I figured it out: this is a four credit class, I broke it down. Four-thousand two-hundred and ninety-eight. Big ones. Well, do you think that what you have to teach me is worth that? Come on, start talking and we'll amortize for each word.

RUTH: You're clearly a bright girl. You can't expect an education to be broken down into monetary terms.

SIMONE: You just did. That's a lot of money, right? It's, like, food for a starving family in a fifth-world country for a year at least. It's

SIMONE: [*Cont'd.*] a car. Well, a used one, anyway. Minus the insurance. Suddenly this number doesn't sound so huge. It's a couple of Armani suits at most. I don't even like Armani. So hey, come on, can't you even say "Yes, Simone, I am worth two Armani suits. I have that to offer you..."

RUTH: I can't say that, no.

SIMONE: No useful skills to be had here.

RUTH: The money doesn't go into my pocket, by the way.

SIMONE: I think it should. It would be more direct that way; you'd feel more of a responsibility. To me. Personally. Don't you think, Dr. Ruth?

RUTH: I'd prefer that you not call me that.

SIMONE: Wrong kind of doctor, man. All you're interested in is a bunch of books written a hundred years ago, and the books written about those books; you're probably writing a book about a book written about a book right now, am I right?

RUTH: If you don't see the connection between books and life, you aren't reading very well. I want you to try. Can you do that? Books might even show you a way to live.

SIMONE: I'm already living, Dr. Ruth. Are you? Because it looks like you haven't changed your hair style in twenty-five years.

RUTH: Well, you weren't even born then, Simone.

SIMONE: Stuck in your best year? Because I see you in a close-cropped, spiky thing.

RUTH: That's enough.

SIMONE: P.S.: You might want to do something about the way you dress.

RUTH: Have you been in therapy?

SIMONE: Don't think that's an original suggestion.

RUTH: I'm not suggesting anything. I simply want to point out that this is not therapy. I am a teacher, not your therapist. You can't just waltz into my office and say whatever hateful thing you please.

SIMONE: I don't know how to waltz.

RUTH: I'm giving up here, Simone. You don't like my class, you don't like me, you want to fail out, I can't stop you.

[RUTH *goes back to her work.* SIMONE *doesn't budge.*]

RUTH: What?

SIMONE: Drew Barrymore would move me.

RUTH: Who?

SIMONE: I think Drew would do it. Getting to meet Drew.

RUTH: Who's Drew Barrymore?

SIMONE: Damn, you really should know these things. She's extremely famous. She's been famous since she was, like, born. I saw her on TV yesterday and she was so real. She connected. You know? You really might relate to your students better if you got a little more up to date.

RUTH: You might be right. But you might not be so behind in class if you spent a little less time watching television.

SIMONE: Drew is a film star, she's in films.

RUTH: You said you saw her on television. Don't you even go to the movies? Probably only the ones that are totally L-Seven. And I know you don't know what that means. [*She forms a square by making an "L" and a "7" with her hands.*]

SIMONE: Square? Anyway, Drew was on TV because she was being interviewed. They have these daytime talk shows nowadays?

RUTH: I've heard of them.

SIMONE: And this chick was in the audience and she started to cry. Because she couldn't believe she was there in the same room with Drew, who's been famous forever, right? She was just, like, sitting there sobbing. And this chick, she had her bleached blond hair pasted down real flat, and she was wearing a rhinestone barrette just like Drew used to, but that whole look is so old Drew, so ten-minutes-ago Drew. The new Drew is sleek and sophisticated and coiffed and this girl, this girl who wanted to be Drew so bad, she wasn't even current.

RUTH: I don't think we're getting anywhere.

SIMONE: And that is so sad. Because the thing about Drew is, she is always changing. It's a constant thing with her, the change.

    And that is, like, what you've got to do... keep moving or you die. Drew knows that. How to invent yourself again and again so you can keep being someone that you like, the someone that you want to be. And once you're it, you've got to move on. Now where was it you were hoping we'd get to?

RUTH: The exam is tomorrow morning at 9 A.M. If you read the material, any of the material, I might actually be able to give you a passing grade. But right now I don't think we need to waste any more of each other's time.

SIMONE: [*Starts to go.*] You might have said that I go to the movies the way you read books. I would have pointed that out, Dr. Ruth.

RUTH: Well I suspect we don't think very much alike.

[SIMONE *goes, turns back.*]

SIMONE: A wall between our souls?

[RUTH *looks at her, about to say something, about to reach out.*]

SIMONE: [*Cont'd.*] I'm sorry if I've been rude. I'm sure a lot of people like your class. Maybe I wasn't raised well. I'm sure somebody's to blame. [SIMONE *goes.*]

RUTH: The next day she showed up at nine on the dot. I felt a certain pride that I had somehow managed to reach her, that she was finally going to make a real effort, but she handed in her blue book after a matter of minutes. I was rather disgusted and let it sit there, until a pile formed on top of it, a pile of blue books filled with the scrawling, down-to-the-last-second pages of my other more eager, or at least more dutiful, students. Later I began to read them straight through from the top, in the order they were stacked in. I wasn't looking forward to Simone's.

    In answering my essay question about how the novel Anna Karenina moves inevitably toward Anna's final tragic act, my students were, for the most part, thorough and precise. They cited all of the events that led to Anna's throwing herself in

RUTH: [*Cont'd.*] front of the train, touching on the many parallel plots and the broader social context. I was satisfied. I felt I had taught well this last semester. My students had learned.

In the blue book she had written "All happy people resemble one another, but each unhappy person is unhappy in their own way." So I guess she had read Anna K.; the opening sentence, at least. My first instinct was to correct the grammar of her little variation. There was nothing else on the page. I flipped through the book; she'd written one more line on the last page: "Any world that I'm welcome to is better than the one that I come from." I'm told it's a rock lyric. Something from the seventies. Anna was written in the seventies, too, funnily enough, a century earlier.

I would have given Simone an F, but I noticed she had already marked down the failing grade herself, on the back of the book. Or maybe the grade was for me.

By the time I came to it, days had passed. I didn't leap to conclusions. Come to think of it, Anna's suicide always takes me by surprise as well, though I've read the novel many times and can map its inexorable progression.

[SIMONE, *just as before...*]

SIMONE: That's a lot of money. Do you think you're worth it? Do you think this class is worth it?

[RUTH *turns to her.*]

RUTH: I live in worlds made by words. Worlds where the dead can speak, and conversations can be replayed, altered past the moment of regret, held over and over until they are bent into new possibilities.

[RUTH *tries to reach toward* SIMONE...]

SIMONE: Do you think I'm worth it? Am I? Am I? Am I?

RUTH: I live there, where death is as impermanent as an anesthesia, and the moment of obliteration is only...a black-out.

[SIMONE *lights a cigarette as lights black out.*]

SIMONE: Ten minutes, time's up — told you I'd be gone by now, baby.

[*The flame illuminates her for a moment, darkness again.*]

J. Rufus Caleb

THE REHEARSAL
A Fantasy

"I know *now* Hendrix was on the set with Little Richard."
— Walter Norcross
owner, Mustang Lounge
Greenville, South Carolina

The Rehearsal: A Fantasy, by J. Rufus Caleb. Copyright © 1995 by J. Rufus Caleb. All rights reserved. Reprinted by permission of John Rufus Caleb and The Radio Stage, WNYC.

CAUTION: Professionals and amateurs are hereby warned that *The Rehearsal: A Fantasy* is subject to a royalty. It is fully protected under the copyright laws of the United States of America and of all countries covered by the International Copyright Union (including the Dominion of Cananda and the rest of the British Commonwealth), and of all countries covered by the Pan-American Copyright Convention and the Universal Copyright Convention, and of all countries with which the United States has reciprocal Copyright relations. All rights, including professional and amateur stage performing, motion picture, recitation, lecturing, public reading, radio broadcasting, television, video or sound taping, all other forms of mechanical or electronic reproduction, such as information storage and retrieval systems and photocopying, and the rights of translation into foreign languages, are strictly reserved. Particular emphasis is laid upon the question of readings, permission for which must be secured from the author's agent in writing.

All inquiries concerning professional, stock, and amateur rights should be addressed to Applause Books, Licensing Division, 1841 Broadway, Suite 1100, New York, NY 10023. No amateur or stock performance or reading of the play may be given without obtaining, in advance, the written permission of Applause Books.

J. Rufus Caleb

In 1973, J. Rufus Caleb joined the faculty of Dickinson College where he taught writing and African-American literature, until 1975, when he moved to the Community College of Philadelphia, where he is an Associate Professor of English, and Director of the Annual Spring Writers Workshop. He has received grants from the Pennsylvania Council on the Arts, the Pennsylvania Humanities Council, and the National Endowment for the Arts.

In 1981, Caleb's play *Benny's Place* received the Eugene O'Neill National Playwrights Conference Theatre Award for "Best Conference Play," as well as other award nominations. It was soon produced for ABC Television, featuring Louis Gossett, Jr. and Cecily Tyson. In 1986, People's Light and Theatre produced *City Lights — An Urban Sprawl*, directed by Murphy Guyer, featuring Ray Aranha and Darryl Edwards. Two years later the Germantown Theatre Guild of Philadelphia commissioned and produced Caleb's *Prologue to Freedom*.

Caleb returned to television in 1989, when WHYY-TV, PBS, Philadelphia produced his play *Jehovah's Witness*. The following year, the New Orleans Center for the Performing Arts staged *Jean Toomer's Cane* (an adaptation of *Cane* by Jean Toomer). *The Devil and Uncle Asa*, commissioned by WNYC Radio Stage, was aired in 1991. *The Devil and Uncle Asa* received the 1993 "Special Achievement Award" from the National Association of Community Broadcasters. In 1992, Caleb was commissioned by New American Radio and Performing Arts to write, direct and produce *The Ballad of Mistuh Jack*. In 1993, Caleb received an NEA grant to write, direct and produce for radio *Moods For Jazz*, an adaptation of *Ask Your Mama: Twelve Moods for Jazz by Langston Hughes*.

Caleb has published fiction and poetry in a number of magazines, including Hoo Doo, Black Series, Journal of Black Poetry, Obsidian, PoetryNOW, Salomé, Shenandoah, Maryland Review and the William and Mary Review.

The Rehearsal: A Fantasy was commissioned for The Radio Stage, a co-production of WNYC, New York Public Radio and the Radio Stage Consortium and broadcast in 1996, by WNYC, produced by Sarah Montague and directed by John Pietrowski. The subsequent stage version of *The Rehearsal* was developed with the assistance of The Playwrights Theatre of New Jersey in 1996.

CHARACTERS

JIMI, nineteen years old

RICHARD, late thirties

SETTING: *A small, cramped juke-joint, in Macon, Georgia. A late, rainy, summer night, 1963.*

A light rises on RICHARD, *stage right, in limbo. He is in profile, facing a pay phone. He is dressed to go on stage. He reaches out towards the phone, stops, drops his hand and shakes his shoulders to settle his jacket on his frame. He pivots to the audience, one hand slicing into his buttoned jacket; the other hand giving a hip gesture. With small movements of his free hand, he could be either counting telephone rings or beats. When he speaks, he jumps into his monologue, addressing hand, initially, and then moves his monologue out to some, indefinite point beyond the audience.*

RICHARD: Art Rupe? This the Art Rupe from Specialty Records? [*Pause.*] Yeah, Art, it's me. Same wonderful Richard. Like a bottle of champagne been laying on its side for a hundred years— but I'm even better, 'cause Richard don't give no hiccups. I ain' going too fast for you, now? I wake you up? Don't tell me you been waitin' up for me to call. [*Coyly.*] How you even know I come back on the scene? Yeah? What he say? Bet he give you a blow-by-blow of the whole show. Excited, was he? Hmmm. 'Bout lovely me? I know you mean he was excited 'bout my playing. I ain' that slow. Of course, I got new material. Bring in a few tunes each stop of the tour. O, no, we playing Macon at the moment. But we ain' but a car ride from Atlanta. Got us booked in a sweet spot. Macon's my hometown, you remember. Go' be jam packed the whole week we there. You understand, Art Rupe, all my friends go' fall by on some one of them nights. Don't want Specialty Records to miss out, being how good together we been in the past. But you know, when Richard go on tour, he can't keep it secret forever. [*Pause.*] I know I disappeared? Dead—who told you that lie? Richard just needed some time off the highlife, after that last world tour. You ain' heard where I been? Well, I started me a little church, way back

RICHARD: [*Cont'd.*] behind Nowhere, Georgia. Had my barber cut down my pretty pompadour. Trimmed my fingernails. And I devoted my life to the ministry: studied, and got ordained. Richard built a fine little church in a little grove of trees. And folks come in droves to hear me preach. Uh-huh, near the whole six years I been off the scene. [*Pause.*] Now, you ain't heard me say I give up music, just the scene. I even took my choir into a studio. Made us a nice little rockin' version of "Walk in the Sunshine." Art Rupe, it ain' yo' fault you missed it. My little gospel record wouldn' a showed on the charts you look at in New York. [*Quickly.*] No, I ain't on a gospel tour. This ain't a gospel tour. Wouldn't be talking to you, Art, was this a gospel tour. [*Pause.*] I put together a band of unknowns. Young boys. Now, don't talk no trash: yeah, they look good, but these boys can play. I spent six months, looking all over the country till I found the right mix. [*Pause.*] O, yes, six years is a long time to be away from the scene. But now I'm back, we go' get together in Macon? Y'know, Art, there ain't been much news outa Specialty since 1957, when I was the news. [*Pause.*] Then who you go' send? O, yeah? But is he coming with his briefcase? O, you definitely excited. Ou-we, my, my, my.

[RICHARD *immediately settles his clothing, shakes down his watch to his wrist, reads the dial, pivots back to the payphone, and begins to dial.*]

[*The light drops.*]

[*A light rises on* JIMI, *downstage center, sitting on a bar stool. A guitar amplifier is nearby. Nothing else is seen.*]

[JIMI *does not have a guitar; and later* RICHARD *will not play the piano. Using their bodies and small gestures, the actors will suggest the instruments, and the music coming from them. The music will be played by two musicians seen in hazy silhouette, from behind a scrim upstage.*]

[JIMI *is preparing to begin a song. The tilt of his torso and the design his fingers make abstractly establish a guitar in his lap. He is focused on his hands in his lap. He nods, his hands having found the place to begin. He launches himself into "Going Home, Tomorrow." He knows the tune perfectly, but he is also exploring, so that as he 'plays' and sings,* JIMI *makes discoveries, nods as he finds ideas he can keep. On occasion, he drops the lyrics and listens to the guitar's notes. But for the flashy print shirt he wears, his persona is the solitary bluesman, anchoring the beat with the heels of both feet, coaxing the music from his instrument. Within this moment,* JIMI *is playing within himself, and playing for himself. Only his voice is heard.*]

JIMI: Going home, tomorrow,

Can't stand your evil ways

Baby, I'm going home, tomorrow

Sick and tired of yo' evil ways.

I'll be better off without you—

I'm in misery all my days.

[JIMI *stops and looks off, left, then fiddles with knobs of his amp. When he begins anew, the wall will light up, and the guitarist will be seen and the guitar heard.*]

JIMI: I'll be better off without you—

I'm in misery all my days.

[*At the bridge,* JIMI's *guitar cries for a few brief moments. He closes the guitar down with the beat of his heel, and launches into the next verse.*]

JIMI: Don't ever try to find me

Don't even call me on the telephone

Hear me, babe, don't ever try to find me,

No need to call me on yo' telephone.

I'm better off without you,

Why don't you leave poor me alone.

[JIMI *repeats the bridge, note for note. However, he stops his heels, while playing. At the last note, his guitar takes off into the realm of pure sound, looking for a way to make the guitar squeal like a saxophone.*]

[*The set lights come up.* RICHARD *is standing, dripping with rain, within a few yards from* JIMI. *He wears a raincoat and a hat.*]

[*When* JIMI *senses, then sees* RICHARD, *he clamps down on his guitar neck.*]

[*For the first time, the steady, summer rain is heard falling on the club's tin roof.*]

[*The lights reveal the cramped OASIS CLUB in Macon, Georgia. However, only the bandstand is emphasized. It is a small platform, with an abused upright piano, electric guitar case, a few music stands, stools. A fullsize tapedeck sits on one stool. Center of the platform is an all purpose amplifier, from which two cables run: one to a wah-wah pedal, and the other off the bandstand, to* JIMI's 'guitar.']

RICHARD: [*taking off hat and coat*] O, don't stop, Jimi. Go on. Ain't nobody said the only thing can be done with a guitar is to play music. Keep on stomping them boats under your ankles. Must still be at least one-two snakes you ain't drove from beneath the floor. I run into a whole slew of 'em snaking out, whilst I'm 'bout to come in the door. Them snakes had they hats and coats on, and mad—disappointed, Jimi. Was talking. man, it's Friday night, my one night off from doing evil in the world, and all I wanna do is slide under the Oasis Club, curl in the dust for a while, but here come some fool banging dirt down on my head. You can tell when a snake mad—don' wiggle, he slide straight, and the smoke just coming outen his ears. I'm curious, so I follow this line o' steamin' snakes, and see 'em duck in under the rinky-dink Midway Bar, which ain't never had no business even being in business. I look down where they going in, 'n' one aft' t'other, they pay they little snake cover charge, go on in. Snake owner put the money in his snake pocket. They order from the kitchen, snake owner put little more money in his snake pocket. You buy a drink, snake money in his pocket. And ever' time he drop money in his pocket, he say 'Thank you, Jimi; thank you, Jimi; thank you, Jimi.'

JIMI: What you talking 'bout, Mistuh Richard?

RICHARD: Maybe you trying not to understand me, Jimi. I'm talking 'bout snakes. Snakes do' like wet. Out in the country—

[JIMI *has turned away; playing a few idle notes.*]

RICHARD: Guess you musta thought I was done talking.

[JIMI *turns immediately back.*]

RICHARD: [*Cont'd.*] Out in the country, when a snake know it go' be a heavy rain, you see 'em sliding up the winda pane.

JIMI: [*Pauses.*] Mistuh Richard. We got snakes in Seattle.

RICHARD: I been to Seattle, Jimi.

JIMI: Snakes don't talk; snakes don't drink in a bar; and they don't smoke out their ears.

RICHARD: Then I must be dumb, huh?

JIMI: Yeah, you think I'm dumb. So you can just tell me a dumb story. It's a dumb story, Mistuh Richard.

RICHARD: What's on your mind, Jimi.

JIMI: [*Deliberate sigh.*] Mister Richard, its four o'clock in the morning.

RICHARD: Tell me something 'bout yourself I don't already know.

JIMI: I been waiting here on this barstool. Just like you told me.

RICHARD: I didn't tell you to rev up that amp.

JIMI: I couldn't just sit here. So I just wanted to hear a little bit of what I was thinking about.

RICHARD: And confused yo'self.

JIMI: I knew where I was going, Mistuh Richard.

RICHARD: But ever'body else was sliding in the opposite direction. How long you had that amp on?

JIMI: I didn't mean to disturb anybody. [*Pauses.*] I didn't even know really if there was anybody else here. I didn't hear nobody.

RICHARD: [*Pauses.*] What would you know—last two hours you been listening to that marble rolling 'round in yo' head. [*Immediately.*] You ain't using the strings I told you to buy. If you throw'd 'way that money, it come right outen—

JIMI: They're in my case. [*Pause.*] You want to see 'em?

RICHARD: I want to hear 'em on your guitar.

JIMI: [*Pause.*] I'll put 'em on, Mistuh Richard. [*Pause.*] Now?

RICHARD: All right, for now, Jimi. All right, for now.

JIMI: [*Pause.*] Mistuh Richard. Where you been?

RICHARD: Now, Jimi, that's not a proper question to ask your employer.

JIMI: [*Nods a few times; then.*] Mistuh Richard, where's my money? C'mon.

RICHARD: That's the question you been waiting to ask, Jimi. Only reason you here, four o'clock in the morning. Otherwise, you'd be out running the streets all night.

JIMI: C'mon, Mistuh Richard, where's my money.

RICHARD: [*Pauses.*] That's what I been doing in that office. Getting some advance money, so's I can put it in your hand.

JIMI: [*Slight whine.*] C'mon, Mister Richard. You paid the whole band right after the show.

RICHARD: 'Cause I stretched my pocket. When I come to your hand, I was down to counting copper Abe Lincolns and a handful of buffaloes. And I know'd you needed bigger money than that. [*Pause.*] So I had to go in an' sweet talk the owner for a while. [*Smiles.*] Walked him right to his car—so he'd understand: even big a star as Richard is, he don't mind getting wet for a club owner what invite Richard in for a week's engagement. Tucked him right in the seat, just like they do in New York.

JIMI: But you got my money, right, Mister Richard?

RICHARD: O, he 'vanced me soon's I asked.

JIMI: [*Pause.*] But I don't see my money, Mister Richard.

RICHARD: I can't just walk in, say money-honey and walk out. He wanted to hear stories.

JIMI: You two could talk tomorrow. At least let me know you're gonna be three hours.

RICHARD: Can't leave the stage, Jimi, till the audience release you. Couldn't do nothing but keep talking. 'N' he lapped up every word. Just like you did. O, gimme more, Mister Richard.

JIMI: I never said that, Mister Richard.

RICHARD: Tell me what it's like to be a star. Back in Seattle? Like my little lap dog, Jimi.

JIMI: All right, Mister Richard. I know all your stories.

RICHARD: Like my little lap dog, Jimi. You remember.

JIMI: Y'know what my favorite of all was? About that teen angel chick. Stripped naked in the back seat of your cadillac. Cruising Norfolk, Virginia for soldiers on leave.

RICHARD: Sailors on leave, Jimi. Git it right.

JIMI: Broke off the daggone rearview mirror trying to get a look.

RICHARD: Was a funny story when I told it.

JIMI: I never thought so.

RICHARD: I should never'a told you that story, Jimi.

JIMI: How the owner like that story?

RICHARD: You don't tell folks down here that motel room stuff. That man 'member when my daddy was 'live. This is my hometown. What's wrong with you?

JIMI: I need to have my money. And you not acting like you gonna give me my money.

RICHARD: And if I propose not to pay you right this minute, what you gon' do—cut my tour again?

JIMI: Uh-huh, I see, Mister Richard. So you not gonna pay me.

RICHARD: And would that not leave you a Seattle Negro in Macon, Georgia. With no money—and no cause to be this deep in Klan country—'cept to play Richard's music. Well, I ain't go' fire you, and I ain't go' not pay you. But I for sure am not gonna pay you till we get done one thing. [Crosses to piano and plays a flurry of notes.]

JIMI: [Pause.] What you talking about, Mistuh Richard?

RICHARD: Boy, you and me gonna have a rehearsal, right here and right now.

JIMI: For what?

RICHARD: Cause I don't like the way you been playing, of course. [*Pause, then bursts.*] This is Richard's tour. You just 'long for music decoration. Any other sideman cut the fool like you, I'd'a fired his butt first time. Wasn't for my pledge to your daddy.

JIMI: Now, Mister Richard, you ain't made no pledge to my daddy.

RICHARD: Was you there when we set eye-on-eye?

JIMI: I'd have known if you'd been talking to him. Well, where you talk to my daddy? He wasn't in Seattle when you came through. I'm the one you talked to. [*Pause.*] 'Bout the big venues you had lined up.

RICHARD: Don't play with me, boy.

JIMI: [*pause*] Yessir, Mister Richard. Yessir. [*Pause.*] Can I have my money now, Mister Richard? And you won't have to worry 'bout me acting up again.

RICHARD: I'm serious. We gonna have a wee-hours in the morning rehearsal. Then you get yo' money.

JIMI: C'mon, Mister Richard, what's going on? I need my money. Places I need to be. I sat on this stool, 'n' you said you'd be right back.

RICHARD: Boy, you want to get paid? Well? Does you or doesn't you?

JIMI: [*Sighs.*] What you want to rehearse?

RICHARD: You don't think I know?

JIMI: I know you know, Mister Richard.

RICHARD: Then wait 'till I tell you. Right now, you get back on the bandstand. You rewind tonight's show tape, like I told you? [*Pause.*] I don't s'pose you listened to it? [*Moves to bandstand.*]

JIMI: Same two chord changes every night.

RICHARD: You ain't even wired the deck. [*Runs tape deck cable into guitar amplifier.*] And it ain't been the same every night. You

RICHARD: [*Cont'd.*] been playing a whole lot more notes than I told you, and you making the rest of us sound raggedy.

JIMI: [*Small jump onto bandstand.*] Hey, Mister Richard, say anything you want, but don't put down my playing. When I lay the sound of my ax on the chicks, the chicks can't dance 'cause they starting to juicy-up.

RICHARD: Don't even talk that trash. You think these "chicks" come to see some no-name Seattle nig-grow play guitar 'tween his legs? Boy, turn on that tape 'fore I forget you got a daddy.

JIMI: [*Turns on deck; quietly.*] I should be getting some credit, too.

RICHARD: Naw, baby, I'm the one had a string o' six hits. You ain' done shit.

[*The show tape kicks in with the band warming up the audience; screaming fans in a small space; guitar out front.*]

RICHARD: [*Cont'd.*] That's me they calling for.

ANNOUNCER [Show tape.]: And now, ladies and gentlemen, live on our stage, himself, the father of rock 'n rhythm, rhythm 'n' soul. Put your hands together for—

RICHARD: [*Screams.*] Me-e-e. Now, I come on stage. And listen to how they love me. O, I love you, too. [*Mimics show tape.*] Thank you, thank you. We-e-e, it's sure good to be back home, in Macon, G-A. All right, now. We gonna ask the band to slow it down a teeny little bit. Here come something from the heart for all my special guests out there.

[*On cue, the show tape band's tempo changes, and it segues into their introduction of "Good-night, Irene." The guitar picks out, and breaks down, the vocal part. The crowd responds. The piano adds a few occasional notes, in punctuation.*]

RICHARD: Right there—lemme jump in, Jimi.

SHOW TAPE RICHARD: All right, let's give that young Seattle boy on guitar a big Macon welcome.

[RICHARD *stops tape.*]

RICHARD: I ain't supposed to be waiting on you to let me play, Jimi.

JIMI: Sometimes you can't help but feel a groove, Mister Richard. Gotta jump on those times. [*Plays a quick burst of notes.*]

RICHARD: Uh-huh. [*Starts tape.*]

[*The show tape guitar continues to break down "Irene," but never loses the melody.*]

SHOW TAPE RICHARD: I don't know what you doing back there, Jimi, but you tearing it up. [*Pause.*] Now c'mon, Jimi, Bring it back home.

[*The show tape guitar loses "Irene" completely, and sounds as if it is saying 'What'? The show tape guitar calls out, hoots, pants.*]

RICHARD: What you doing behind my back, boy?

JIMI: Aw, Mister Richard, you should'a turned around.

RICHARD: And be part of yo' audience? I be damned.

[*The show tape guitar illustrates* JIMI's *monologue. Periodically,* JIMI's *rehearsal guitar adds a new layer of notes.*]

JIMI: I wasn't tryin' to be the show. This girl in the corner of the floor was the show. I tried to get you to look. 'Mistuh Richard, Mistuh Richard, look'a that girl out there.' I lost some notes trying to get your attention. I couldn't keep my eyes off her from the time she walked in the door. She was just moving, moving, squeezing hands, kissing cheeks and moving to the stage. Then she's dropping a little purse in his hand, and he must be her old man. She's in the corner. I aim my ax right at her, but I know: Aw, girl, you don' need me. You don't even need the drummer to groove. Don' lie to me. You playing with me, girl, you playing with me. All right. There's where I jumped in and played all over her: O, look'a her out there with that cherry red dress on. O, don't she know, don't she know, how to shake her thang. [*Pause.*] She's just grooving now, Mister Richard, climbing up my notes, her big coconuts shaking in her dress. Then she kinda cups 'em up, and just throws 'em out her dress. And quick as a dream, she tucks those mountains back. Now here she come slinking, slinking, slinking to the neck o' my ax. Aw, come on girl, throw your head back, let your eyes roll back in delight. Look'a that girl, shining cherry red. O, my.

JIMI: [*Cont'd.*] O, my, girl. And there. I'm lowering down my guitar. Gonna pick you right up, wrapped in the hot sides of your thighs. O, chile, lemme take you, and I take her, and I take her. And I take her.

RICHARD: [*Stops tape.*] Boy, I don't know where in the white wilderness of Seattle you learned that. But tonight, you will unlearn it. [*Starts the tape.*]

[*The space left by the guitar is taken by the piano, which picks out the crisp opening notes of "Irene." The rest of the band, with guitar, follows and settles into the even rhythm. The Introduction does begin to drive, but the arrangement is mechanical.* RICHARD *listens intently to the tape;* JIMI's *mind is wandering.*]

RICHARD: [*Continues; humming.*] Finally, you sounding like you can count.

JIMI: Aw, Mister Richard, I just wanna make my music.

RICHARD: [*Humming.*] Have to be able to read music to write music.

JIMI: Why you want to start that again.

RICHARD: Well, can you can, or can you can't read music? Don't know why your daddy ain't teach you to read. Wonder, he figure you too dumb—there. Listen. You making mistakes. And your A-string's gone flat. But you just playing on.

[*The show tape continues with* RICHARD's *vocals rendering the verses.* RICHARD *is listening to everything, mimicking various instruments, passing judgment with his body or guttural sounds. "Irene' ends in applause.* RICHARD *turns off tape, angrily.*]

RICHARD: 'Nough of you playing the fool. Aw-right, we gonna take it from the top—or what s'posed to been the top.

JIMI: We going through the whole show?

RICHARD: Yessir. From 'good evening' to 'good night.' Just like I wrote the show.

JIMI: [*Flash of anger.*] That show's two hours. You must be crazy.

RICHARD: Naw, I'm the boss. [*Explodes.*] Nigga, I got deals riding on

RICHARD: [*Cont'd.*] this comeback tour. So don't mess with me. You think we playing for some hussy in a red dress. So you can lay in the crack of some girl you can buy for a fried fish sandwich? This tour's for them two slack-eye white boys was here for the show. An' before we went on, I 'specially looked at you Jimi, and tol' yo' simple self: what go into these white boy ears tonight is important. They from New York. And the only white folks come this deep south is important white folks. 'N' Jimi, you even nodded and grinned like you understood me. So what happen when the show's over? I jump off the bandstand, and they gone. Just gone. [*Pause.*] So, if yo' guitar is plugged in, despite yo' brain, pick up the beat and stay with me. We go' watch the sun rise from the woodshed. One-two-three. One-two-three.

[RICHARD *and* JIMI *play the introduction to* "*Irene.*"]

RICHARD: [*Cont'd.*] All right, now. You settling into the groove. [*Pause.*] I want you to leave off playing under the verses; come in on the chorus.

[JIMI *stops.* RICHARD *stops.*]

JIMI: Well, Mister Richard, what's the point of me playing at all, if I'm just gonna strum like a banjo?

RICHARD: 'Cause I prefer to go for a different sound.

JIMI: Just your piano.

RICHARD: O, no, my piano ain't go' be holding y'all together on this one. Richard just go' sing on "Irene." What I'm looking for is for everybody to just rock 'long: da—da—da; da—da—da. Build off that. Then I jump in with the drum, conga, and bass.

JIMI: Why I have to drop out?

RICHARD: You back in on the chorus.

JIMI: [*Edge.*] Well why we not practicing with the others?

RICHARD: They don't need to rehearse. They parts don't change. I'll keep you company for now. You ready?

JIMI: [Pause.] And you gonna pay me when we get done, right, Mister Richard?

RICHARD: That's the onliest deal you go' get, Jimi.

JIMI: But we don't have to do the whole show, right Mister Richard? I do have someplace I'm supposed to be.

RICHARD: Well, Jimi, I need you to play better.

JIMI: All right, Mister Richard.

[RICHARD *cues* JIMI *with notes. Both play the exact Introduction.*]

RICHARD: [*Exact delivery as on show tape.*] Thank you, thank you. Aw right, now, here come something from the heart. [*Pause.*] Saturday night we got married/ Me and my wife settled down/ Now me and my wife we're parking/ Gonna take another stroll downtown. [*Beat.*] Irene, good night/ Irene, good night—well, sing, Jimi.

RICHARD/JIMI: Irene, good night/ Good night, Irene/ I'll see you in my dreams.

[RICHARD *and* JIMI *play the bridge.*]

RICHARD: [*Pause.*] To the bridge. Shom—da—da—boom.

Both stop on the note.

RICHARD: [*Continues.*] Well? What you think?

JIMI: [*Playing a B. B. King riff.*] I guess it's different.

RICHARD: Not the note, boy. I mean can you see the feeling I'm after. The colors.

JIMI: [*Another riff.*] Mister Richard, I just can't get into this hillbilly waltz music.

RICHARD: Jimi, yo' job is to get into it.

JIMI: [pause] I hear you tonight, I'm thinking you could go higher than Robert Johnson. You got the voice for some blues, Mistuh Richard.

RICHARD: What you know 'bout blues? You ain't even got a sense of humor.

JIMI: Then what was I doing in Seattle? I know my blues, Mister Richard.

RICHARD: Say who?

JIMI: Albert King, that's who.

RICHARD: Where you play with some Albert King?

JIMI: [*Pause.*] In St. Louis.

RICHARD: When your butt ever sit in St Louis.

JIMI: [*Pause.*] You don't know everywhere I've been, Mr. Richard.

RICHARD: I may not've been there when your mama dropped you off in the world, but since then I know you been in Seattle and on my band bus.

JIMI: So you wanna think.

RICHARD: Them two weeks? O, you wanna claim you was in St. Louis.

JIMI: Mostly. I went to some other places on the way.

RICHARD: You lying. You was shacked up with that goofy country girl what followed you 'round in Greenville.

JIMI: [*Slyly.*] I just told the fellas that.

RICHARD: Why you lie? What—you think I was go' come running after you?

JIMI: I couldn't tell *what* you were going to do.

RICHARD: [*Pauses fully; slowly.*] Then you should'a checked yo' ID. Now is probably when you lying. You shack up with whoever you want.

JIMI: I swear, Mistuh Richard; I saw Albert King—sitting in Arch Recording.

RICHARD: Arch Recording!?

JIMI: [*Pause; smiles.*] In the lobby. Mister Albert was just sitting there, plugged into this nice little amp, driving his ax like a freight train. [*Guitar burst, similar to one at open, on "Going Home."*]

[JIMI *moves into the limbo area, as the light there rises on a low stool. He cradles his guitar upright.*]

[JIMI *approaches the stool, reverentially.*]

JIMI: I got as close to him as I could. I was trying to see his finger-work, while he was leaning over his ax, checking out my shoes.

[JIMI *bends towards* ALBERT'*s left hand. Then he pivots in* RICHARD'*s direction and personifies* ALBERT, *playing soundlessly, and checking out* JIMI'*s shoes.*]

RICHARD: He like them shoes?

[ALBERT *"approves" of the shoes.*]

JIMI: Then Mistuh Albert looked up, real perplexed, surprised. [*Sits on stool, tilts his head up to*] You colored. Don't think I ever seen a colored boy wear shoes like them. I just nodded. Then he said: Son, you make a better door than a window. I'm just standing there, staring at his hand after he stopped playing. So he just pushed me a little to the side and said: I got to keep an eye out for the man. I asked 'What man'? And he asked me: What's in there, Sonnyboy—meaning my guitar case. I'm still so knocked out that it's Albert King, I say, 'My guitar.' He cracked up, and I felt real stupid. But he told me: Sit on down. He meant what kind of guitar do I play. I'm opening up my case, and he goes: You must be in love, Sonnyboy, 'cause that's some kin'a shirt you got on. Go' git me one, next time I'm passing through Puerto Rico, France. I knew what he was gonna ask next: Can you play. [*Over to Richard.*] And he didn't mean can I play the guitar.

RICHARD: Can you play it.

JIMI: [*Doing a mock tuning.*] I could tell he liked me, but he wasn't going to loan me his guitar cord. "A strong man may not need a zipper to get ready, but a bluesman—

JIMI & RICHARD: —better have his long black snake. Sonnyboy, plug into that empty socket, and light up.

JIMI: I surprised him, and went way back to his first album. I wasn't gonna put one note in Mistuh Albert's ear but what I learned from his album.

[JIMI *plays and the music heard* is *the blues, but with a nod to the polished surface of rhythm and blues. The music is cousin to B B King: ironic, sly, with mocking pauses. Who the mockingbird be is*

clear—but who is the mock-ee? The music is distant cousin to B. B. King: full, broad notes, ornate, even riddled with random riffs: gut, guttural, all down in the gutter. JIMI *plays on a delicate blues.* JIMI *is winding down the music.*]

JIMI: Yeah, put the baby to bed, Sonnyboy. Turn off the light. And tip-toe. Out the. Room. [JIMI *releases the strings, clamps down on the neck.*] Then he said: O, you didn't have to be that nice to my stuff, Sonnyboy. And for a while, that's *all* he said. Then he just started showing me all kinds of stuff with his ax. How to anchor the guitar with my elbow, so I can pick different strings with both hands. To re-tune on the fly, and when to do it so that that stretching string folds right into the music. [*Reveling.*] You know, Mistuh Albert's got these big hands, like me, and he can wrap 'em 'round the neck, and make 'em go like pistons. He don't even use a pick.

RICHARD: Who don't know 'bout Albert crusty thumbnail?

JIMI: And he plays upside-down and left-handed, too.

RICHARD: And I know that. [*Pause.*] Albert ask after me? [*Pause.*] O, you ain't tell Albert you worked for me?

JIMI: [*Pause.*] After a while

RICHARD: [Quickly.] What chu tell him?

JIMI: He asked what you had in the set. [*Pause; smiles.*] He said, "Good-night, Irene" was too country for him.

RICHARD: Albert ain't call *me* country. Albert from too deep in Mississippi to call *me* country.

JIMI: [*Edge of condescension.*] We weren't talking about you. We just agreed that for 1963, "Irene" just too country.

RICHARD: You can't tell a whole note from a fly on the wall, but you will arrange my set.

JIMI: We were talking about Leadbelly.

RICHARD: What *you* have to say 'bout Leadbelly?

JIMI: I'd heard about him, Mister Richard.

RICHARD: Well then, I wanna hear.

JIMI: He was real big, real country and a real bad man.

RICHARD: All right, you know some Leadbelly.

JIMI: [*Warming.*] Near the whole of his adult life, the state of Louisiana would run him in and out of jail for shooting folks.

RICHARD: [*Amused.*] You talking Albert King now.

JIMI: Uh-huh. Mister Albert says Leadbelly had him a pistol called a left-handed Wheeler. Made from magnet metal. And he would stick that left-hand Wheeler right 'gainst his Leadbelly, 'stead of a holster. And when he died, the undertaker pulled enough bullets out of Leadbelly's gut to line his coffin. [*Shrugs.*] Hard to believe *that's* the man that wrote "Goodnight, Irene."

RICHARD: You don't know Albert jiving you with them tall tales?

JIMI: Mr. Albert was showing me something. How Leadbelly started out with something special, only he lost it. [*Pause.*] Mister Albert says I got something special, too. And I told him, don't worry 'bout me: I'm going to keep my special thing.

RICHARD: Leadbelly and Jimi occupying the same sentence?

JIMI: I won't ever write some slow-drag "Goodnight, Irene.

RICHARD: [*Pause.*] Lemme tell you one more story 'bout "slow-drag Leadbelly." One of them times he was in Angola Prison, the gov'nor of the state of Louisiana, Huey P. Long—ever hear o' the kingfisher? Thought not. Well Kingfisher sent word in to Leadbelly: Write me a song, and I will set you free. But the warden say: Wait a minute, Gov'nor, Leadbelly in for life this time. We gotta cure this colored man of killing taxpayers. So Kingfisher sent another word in to Leadbelly: I better like that song; otherwise, you don't walk. Leadbelly got to thinking, got to working. Wrote out "Irene," the first night, and put that pretty tune here in his back pocket. Then he wrote six more tunes he know'd was dogs. Sent 'em up the gov'nor's mansion, one-at-a-time. And each time Kingfisher throw'd a dog in the trash, that warden show'd Leadbelly his red neck. [*Pause.*] You understand what I mean by "showing his red neck," don't chu? Even a Seattle Negro must'a heard what that mean.

JIMI: [*Thoughtfully.*] Yessir, Mister Richard.

RICHARD: All right, you listening. Well, when Leadbelly was ready, he sent out "Irene." And damn if he ain't walk a free man soon's the Kingfisher could tap out the notes to the words. Call Leadbelly country, and more bad news than a nightmare—but he was slick, too.

JIMI: I bet he was sweating scared.

RICHARD: He know'd what he was doing.

RICHARD: You can know what you're doing and still be scared.

RICHARD: What you doing to be scared 'bout?

JIMI: I'm not talking 'bout me. What if that Kingfisher had thrown "Irene" in the trash, too?

RICHARD: Like you would'a, huh?

JIMI: Well, Mister Richard? You get your stuff right and send it out there and you got your whole life depending on it.

RICHARD: [*Pause.*] You better have more'n your 'special stuff' to depend on. You better know what you doing.

JIMI: I know what I'm doing.

RICHARD: No, you don't, Jimi. Did you know, you wouldn't'a run from me to a few sessions with Albert. Lucky I took you back.

JIMI: I knew you would. 'Cause you know what you doing, what you got.

RICHARD: Albert planning to give you more work? [*Pause.*] How much he paying you for a session?

JIMI: I didn't say I got a job with Mister Albert.

RICHARD: O, I see. I'm still the onliest one to offer you some real work. So, what kind o' stuff Mister Laundromat Blues doing at Arch?

JIMI: We didn't talk about that.

RICHARD: His stuff so secret, he ain't let you listen from the booth? [*Pause.*] Well then, what Albert say 'bout his deal?

JIMI: Nothing.

RICHARD: Laundromat? And didn't go on and on 'bout his deal?

JIMI: Don't always have to be 'bout business, Mister Richard.

RICHARD: What else but?

JIMI: [*Pause.*] Mister Albert understands what it's about.

RICHARD: Since when?

JIMI: [*With some poignancy.*] The blues is about playing what you done lived, so everybody what hear yo' blues, got to live it, too. How you wake up so lonely in the morning, you make a deal with the devil, just to talk to somebody on the phone. The blues is sadness, pain and sorrow so deep down in a black man's soul . . .

RICHARD: Aw, Jimi, that's the stuff Albert s'posed to say when they put you on the TV not what he said when they put him on the TV that one time. Lord'a'mercy. [*Pause.*] I bet you wore that same Honolulu shirt you tried to wear tonight. Ha. And them stingy-crotch blue jeans you think you look so good in.

JIMI: What you driving at, Mister Richard. [*Meekly.*] What?

RICHARD: [*Begins laughing.*] I know Albert take one look at you and saw a Seattle nig-row, who ain't know'd but 'bout six colored people growing up, and what learned all the little he know about colored music from the half-dozen 'blues' records some white deejay choose to let him hear.

JIMI: You don't know what Mister Albert was thinking.

RICHARD: I know he talk to you like you was a white boy.

JIMI: I don't have to grow up eating hominy grits on some plantation to play the blues, Mister Richard.

RICHARD: Who told you that?

JIMI: Well then, to play my blues. I'm telling you the truth, Mister Albert says I got something special in my hands. I just gotta find a way to get it out.

RICHARD: [*Shakes head.*] So you can be like Albert—sitting in that lobby throwing out every new note he got, sweating the varnish off his guitar. Hoping some doped-up or drunked-up slack-eye white man give him a contract. But he ain't giving out no contracts to colored to sing the blues. He waiting for some more

RICHARD: [*Cont'd.*] white boys to learn to play it. Look what been done with Elvis. Ain't give Elvis a contract to sing hillbilly. Elvis just happen to be the first singing cracker to come 'long when Sam Phillips put out the word that could he find him a good-looking white boy could sound like a 'nigger' he could make a million dollars. Shoot, let's go on to the second verse, 'fore I forget you got a daddy out there somewhere. Pick up the bridge.

[*Piano and guitar hit the bridge exactly.*]

RICHARD: [*Continues; hums few bars of verse.*] Wait for me. I'm trying something. [*Hums entire verse, exactly as on tape.*] All right now. [*Pause.*] Sometimes I run to the country, babe/ Sometimes I roam downtown/ Sometimes I take a great notion/ To jump in the river and drown. [Pause.] Everybody, go—

RICHARD & JIMI: Irene good night/ Irene good night/ Good night Irene/ Good night Irene/ I'll see you in my dreams.

[JIMI'*s angry guitar solo overtakes the bridge, and begins to drive.*]

RICHARD: Don't drift, boy.

[JIMI *stops.*]

JIMI: Elvis got his contract because kids don't want to hear Pat Boone no more. Man, Elvis scares them middle-class old folk.

RICHARD: That what they tell you back in Seattle? Elvis come on the scene when slack-eye couldn't put over Pat Boone doing covers of Little Richard songs. Missed on Pat, went on and hired Elvis, to cover Big Mama Thornton's "Hounddog."

JIMI: Aw, Mister Richard, you know Elvis can sing.

RICHARD: He don't need a colored boy to broadcast that. You know what Elvis say: "All nigras can do for me is shine my shoes and buy my records." [*Pause.*] Well, is it is, or is it ain't?

JIMI: Mister Richard, that don't sound like Elvis.

RICHARD: I know it don't to you.

JIMI: He talks all the time about listening to Negro music growing up. Just because he's from the south don't mean he's prejudiced. It's 'cause you're from the south you think like that.

RICHARD: You right, there.

JIMI: You just jealous, 'cause Elvis' stuff is a hit.

RICHARD: And I ain't had the hits? And back on the scene for some more.

JIMI: [*Pause.*] Elvis got the stuff everybody want to see.

RICHARD: O, I see. [*Picks out notes.*] Like the little stuff you got, huh?

JIMI: [*Eager.*] You wrong, Mister Richard, my stuff's big and plentiful.

RICHARD: Mmmm, goodness, this boy think he got a package.

JIMI: I know I can play better'n Elvis. And shoot, when I get my shot, I'm'a make Elvis' hips look as tame as Pat Boone's shoes. [*Plays a fast, hard riff.*]

RICHARD: So you think feeling up a guitar go' get it? Like you claim it does for these little colored girls.

JIMI: Damn right it does. And I'm gonna fire up the white chicks with the same stuff.

RICHARD: Boy, they ain't go' let you do yo' raunchy stuff 'fore little white girls.

JIMI: I was already doing my stuff back in Seattle. And all there was were white chicks.

RICHARD: Now, Jimi, you wasn't doing all that dirty stuff in Seattle. You even got the chance to unbutton your shirt 'cause them little girl daddys wasn't watching.

JIMI: Shoot, Mister Richard, nobody was worried 'bout that stuff. You been dealing with these crazy Georgia rednecks too long. This place ain't even America, really.

RICHARD: [*Pause.*] I'm just trying to teach you some things, Jimi, that your daddy neglected.

JIMI: [*Fast, hard riff, directed at* RICHARD.] I believe the truth is, you don't got nothing to teach me. I could take *you* places.

RICHARD: Now I know yo' daddy, and I know he taught you more respect than you showing.

JIMI: What's he gonna teach me in a three minute phone call from on the road? I've been putting my stuff together all by myself.

RICHARD: Jimi, Jimi, Jimi. Slack-eye ain' go' be able to do nothing with your stuff.

JIMI: He won't have a choice. Mister Richard, you know I'm good.

RICHARD: O, you got some talent. But it take more'n that to make a package.

JIMI: I'm gonna get my contract, Mister Richard. Then I'm gonna blow everybody's mind with my record. You saw my stuff back in Seattle, and you dug it like everybody else. Then you hired me on the spot.

RICHARD: 'Cause you could play guitar, and on the rare occasion when I needed something a little special, I could teach you to deliver. Jimi, the onliest thing different slack-eye go' let out there is a package like Elvis on the one side and me on the other side. Nothing else go' squeeze through the door—least not for the big time contract that's gleaming in your eye. I wasn't brought up to dress in those costumes I wear on stage. My people don't even want me to sing the very songs I wrote. I'm nothing but the devil on stage. I know that. And I'll tell you something, boy: Had I my will and my way, I'd be singing the Lord's music on this tour. But I'm the first king of rock 'n' rhythm. When I got the urge six years ago to sing what I ought to [*Gentle, gospel phrasing.*] I had to jump my own world tour to do it. Back then every color of people was crazy 'bout my rock 'n' rhythm. Nineteen-hundred-and-fifty-seven, headlining a world tour. We had played Japan. And had filled a giant airplane hangar in Manila.

[JIMI's *guitar, with spare, resonant notes, joins* RICHARD's *phrasing.*]

'Bout to wrap up Sydney, Australia. But that evil Russian man put up his sputnik in the air, and like to scare the life out the world. And that very night was the only time my daddy come to me in a dream. Stood the foot of my bed and tell me, I was making music for evil. Was all he said. Son—

[*Both arrive at the same note.*]

RICHARD: [*Cont'd.*] — you making music for evil. Here I'm the father of rhythm 'n' rock. String of hits, and the very next morning I get on a cross country bus out'a Sydney, going north. I didn't care where, I don't know why. Once we leave the city behind, that bus started to pass all manner of brown people 'long the way. They would smile right up to Richard in that bus, and wave; Richard smile right back out the window, and shake a little wave down on 'em. Bus drove me through a scrubbrush desert, up an endless mountain, till it rolled down into the smell of the dank sea. And the Lord, he stopped that bus and took me off—just like the Lord, he had put me on a bus in the first place. Here, Richard, dwell amongst these little brown people. Dead of night, weren't nobody 'round. But Richard walked, down a dirt road, that could have been any country road in any country—with just 'nough moonlight to see ahead. [*Pause.*] I begin hearing this sound. A kind'a 'wang-wang" A sound like could be made on a Jews-harp. Or like that thing you can do with the pedal.

[RICHARD *creates the sound of a didgeridoo. He shakes his hands, and he makes a steady drone.*]

[JIMI *processes a note through the wah-wah pedal.* JIMI *creates the sound of the didgeridoo. He captures the gentle sameness of its sound, and at the same time lets us know that* RICHARD *is walking closer to the source of that energy.*]

[RICHARD *adds his hands clapping.*]

RICHARD: I was sure it was God setting the night a-buzz. [*Pause.*] I come a little closer and hear the beating of sticks-on-sticks. And there they all was, in a clearing, lit by torchfires. Hundreds of brown people and I'm watching. Watching a dance I could not comprehend. Men in pointed caps, who writhed on the ground like snakes. Women with exposed breasts, who acted like men. Men who were women. Men with feathers covering they bodies. And all throughout, the air smelled of blood, sweat and the dank sea.

[JIMI *stops playing.*]

[RICHARD *creates the* didgeridoo, *and takes us out of that night.*

Again JIMI *comes in under him, and relieves him of the music. Jimi adds various touches to the sound, that reflect the next part of* RICHARD*'s monologue.*]

[JIMI*'s guitar carries* RICHARD *back to the piano; he sits.*]

RICHARD: [*Chuckling.*] Come morning, they talking to me, but I don't understand a word they was saying. When they realize I couldn't, they kind'a drew back from me. So, Richard give 'em his signature, to pull 'em right back. [*Shakes out his hands.*] Lord, don't they give Richard his signal right back. Then they looked at each other, and shrugged. They didn't know who Richard was. Even the ones what spoke English didn't know me. Had not one of my records. I come to find out, all night, they was thinking I'm somebody son or brother what done come back home for this special ceremony.

[RICHARD *lays down a series of happy gospel notes.* JIMI *bends his sound to echo* RICHARD*'s notes. But with the shift in* RICHARD*'s monologue,* JIMI*'s guitar becomes bluer and bluer.*]

RICHARD: Seem like for a month, I'm singing my church songs to them; they singing they religious chants to me. O, we was having a joyous time. [*Pause; stops playing.*] But slack-eye found me, as far in that outback as I was. Pull up in a big French car, covered with wanted posters: "Have you seen this man." "The king of rock 'n' rhythm done run 'way." O, slack-eye pulled on me, and he pulled on me. You letting everybody down. Gonna miss the high-life, and the big paychecks. Called me madman, gonna call the FBI and put me in jail. Made it so Richard had to go back. But soon's that tour was done, got on another bus, back to Macon, back to the little church what give me my first life. [*Pauses.*] Only the money is so good. And the whole time I was off the scene, my fans was sending me they love through the mail. [*Pauses.*]

[JIMI *fills the space with a pure blues. Clear, clean notes, without irony, without lyrics to shape our response, to filter the pain.* JIMI *is drifting, and with a note placed here and there,* RICHARD *"flags" the places* JIMI *discovers.*]

RICHARD: [*Cont'd.*] I'll tell you one thing, Jimi: many a night I've

RICHARD: [*Cont'd.*] lied awake on this tour, my soul torn in two, hoping my daddy'd come and show his face again. [*Pauses.*] You ever hear, that when you gone, supposed to cross your shadow on the foot of the bed of somebody you close to? [*Pause.*] Daddy never throw'd his shadow 'cross my mama's bed. The dead s'posed to do that, ever'body say so. [*Pauses.*] Long gone, these twenty-five years, he never throw'd his shadow 'cross the foot of mama's bed. [*In rhythm.*] Not nair', one sign, good-bye. Left her 'lone, crying on the deep-down ache in her head. [*Pauses.*]

[JIMI *continues, deeply lost in his blues phrasing.* JIMI *is only a conduit for the notes.*]

RICHARD: [*Continues.*] Nice, Jimi.

[RICHARD *hums a few bars, then scats along, feelingly and leading the guitar's phrasing.*]

[*Voice and guitar come together as if rehearsed.* RICHARD *is intent on the intense* JIMI, *hunched over his guitar.*]

RICHARD: [*Drifting into his private world, then in rhythm.*]

Ever hold a man

so close

smell the gin

cigarette

the blood

bubbling from his throat

cause he has been shot down

by his best friend

ove' a twenty-cent glass

of gin.

When you coming home, daddy

When you coming back, tonight

Will you give me some sugar

in the morning

RICHARD: [*Cont'd.*] Is you ever go' do right.

Was a low-roof juke-joint place

Way back in the devil's woods.

[*Stops abruptly.*]

[JIMI's *guitar repeats the lines, then continues through the verse's resolution. He fills the space with a flurry of notes, extends the phrasing.*]

RICHARD: Jimi? [*Grasps* JIMI's *knee.*] Jimi? [*Slowly.*] Was my daddy what died that way, Jimi. I saw that nickel-plate coming out. Knew what it was, 'cause I'd seen it so many times before. Then I saw it go 'pop.' My daddy come stumbling over to me. Need to get over to me. Pulled me down to the floor. Like we could'a been wrestling. Died with my eyes on his face. Here I am, a lad of ten, tagging 'long 'hind his daddy. Lord'a mercy, my long gone daddy. [*Recovering composure.*]

[JIMI's *guitar 'repeats'* RICHARD's *last sentence, syllable-for-syllable.* JIMI's *guitar repeats the first phrase of its phrasing of* RICHARD's *sentence, with embellishment. The guitar plays a set of spare random notes. The guitar is stuck.*]

JIMI: C'mon, Mister Richard. Gimme something to work on. [JIMI *is excited, scared and desperate.*] We got something going. Where we going, Mistuh Richard. C'mon, Mistuh Richard, take it. [*Trails off playing.*] Mister Richard? [*Realizes* RICHARD's *hand on his knee, and springs off his stool.*] Keep your hands off me.

RICHARD: My daddy usta grab my leg like that, when I done something that tickled him. Strongest thing I remember—

JIMI: [*Intense.*] I told you before, I ain't no faggot.

RICHARD: I just wanted to touch somebody. [*Open and vulnerable.*] Wasn't you listening to me? Wasn't touching you that way.

JIMI: I was playing. Trying to find something. And I almost got it.

RICHARD: I heard you, Jimi. You was there right with me. I just... [*Shrugs.*]

JIMI: You ruined it.

RICHARD: We can get it back, Jimi.

JIMI: We? I was doing it. Staying out the way. Letting it come.

RICHARD: Here's what you was doing. [*Poised to play; cannot remember.*]

JIMI: [*Pauses.*] I'll get it back.

[JIMI *retrieves guitar case, and opens it on floor. He unplugs his guitar, and as a ritual, kisses its neck quickly and nestles it into the case.*]

RICHARD: [*A little shaken.*] What you doing, Jimi? Now, now, we ain't done. Whole lot more o' this tape to do.

[JIMI *unplugs his small amp from the larger band amp, begins to coil the two cables and tape the loops. When he is done, he will have a small pile of possessions.*]

JIMI: I'm done, Mister Richard. I want the money I earned for two weeks work.

RICHARD: [*Placating.*] I tol' you, I got your money, Jimi. [*Pause.*] Won't be no more loans coming.

JIMI: I won't need none.

RICHARD: Go on 'n' spend it on whatever hussy you got waiting.

JIMI: I'm not going to no girl. Why you keep saying that. I almost never bother with those girls hanging 'round. Mister Richard, when I'm not in one of these bars playing, I'm back in whatever cheap room you got me in—creating my music. I hear you all talking about me in the morning. If you don't hear me, it's cause I don't need to plug in my amp to hear what I'm playing. [*Finishes piling.*]

RICHARD: [*Tentatively.*] Where you going, Jimi.

JIMI: [*Pause.*] To the bus station.

RICHARD: [Weary.] Jimi, don't play with me.

JIMI: I'm going to New York City, Mister Richard.

RICHARD: Boy, you going' where?

JIMI: [*Pauses.*] Mister Richard, I'm going to be on the Ed Sullivan

JIMI: [*Cont'd.*] Show. He don't know it yet. He don't even know my name yet, but you watch. I'm gonna do exactly what Mister Albert did: be patient. Plug in and fire up right in the lobby.

RICHARD: You can't do that country stuff in New York City. I been there. Country only works in the country.

JIMI: Just because you can't, doesn't mean I can't. I'm gonna get a crowd of 'em 'round me, and show 'em all my tricks. And when I do get my shot, I'm gonna play all over the place. Play some blues like they ain't never heard before.

RICHARD: Shoot, you be back to my tour. The little money I got for you barely carry you past the subway.

JIMI: I'm not coming back this time, Mister Richard.

RICHARD: [Pause.] Jimi, I can't get 'long 'out a guitar.

JIMI: What about when I was in St. Louis?

RICHARD: I didn't bring you clear 'cross the country, cause I could not find a guitar player.

JIMI: So you know. [*Pause.*] Mister Richard, you owe me something. For what I can do; for what I did for you on this tour. [*Shrugs.*] But I'm always the one who's got to pay. [*Pause.*] You said you have my money. I got someplace to be, Mistuh Richard.

RICHARD: [*Suspicious.*] What them slack-eyes from New York promise you, Jimi?

JIMI: I don't know what you talking about, Mister Richard.

RICHARD: [*Bit nervous.*] You lying to me, boy. They ain't come all this way, and just disappear the same night. I been huntin' they damn asses all over Macon—Naw, if they wanted your stuff, they'd give'd you bus fare. [*Pause.*] All right, Jimi. All right.

[RICHARD *pulls out money clip; counts out one-hundred-twenty dollars, which he hands to* JIMI. RICHARD *pivots back to face piano.* JIMI *pockets the money, loads up his stuff, surveys for anything overlooked.*]

JIMI: Mister Richard. This is more than I need for bus fare.

RICHARD: That's yours, Jimi. And you will need every penny, and a hundred times more. I just missed with you, Jimi.

[JIMI *nods.* RICHARD *shakes a wave.* JIMI *exits, closing the door softly.*]

RICHARD: Well, well, well. Well, well. Ev'body long gone. [*Tickles the keyboard; begins to pick out "Goodnight, Irene," in a bluesy/gospel tone, toying with the verse; sings.*] Stop gambling and rambling all over town/Stop staying out late every night/Come home to your wife and your family/And dine by the fireside bright. [*Continues through chorus.*] Sometimes I live in the country, babe/Sometimes I live downtown/Sometimes I take a great notion/To jump in the river and drown. [*Trailing off.*] Irene, good night/Irene, good night/Good night, Irene/Good night, Irene/I'll see you in my dreams.

THE END

Edward de Grazia

THE VACUUM CLEANER

An Opera in One Act

The Vacuum Cleaner by Edward de Grazia. Copyright © 1997 by Edward de Grazia. All rights reserved. Reprinted by permission of the author.

CAUTION: Professionals and amateurs are hereby warned that *The Vacuum Cleaner* by Edward de Grazia is subject to a royalty. It is fully protected under the copyright laws of the United States of America, and of all countries covered by the International Copyright Union (including the Dominion of Canada and the rest of the British Commonwealth), and of all countries covered by the Pan-American Convention and the Universal Copyright Convention, and of all countries with which the United States has reciprocal copyright relations. All rights, including professional, amateur, motion picture, recitation, lecturing, public reading, radio broadcasting, television, video or sound taping, all other forms of mechanical or electronic reproduction, such as information storage and retrieval systems and photocopying, and the rights of translation into foreign languages, are strictly reserved. Particular emphasis is placed upon the question of readings, permission for which must be secured from the author's agent in writing.

All inquiries concerning professional, stock, and amateur rights should be addressed to Applause Books, Licensing Division, 1841 Broadway, Suite 1100, New York, NY 10023. No amateur or stock performance or reading of the play may be given without obtaining, in advance, the written permission of Applause Books.

Edward de Grazia

Edward de Grazia took his law degree to Washington, D.C. where he practiced at the F.C.C. bar, did what little was in his power to combat McCarthyism, wrote book reviews for the *New York Times* and *Washington Post*, and alerted the press of the country to the operation of federal literary censors when he went to court to save a rare-edition copy of Aristophanes' *Lysistrata* from being destroyed as obscene by the U.S. Post Office Department. This marked the beginning of the end of the censorship of literature and art by Post Office officials, a practice de Grazia described and documented in the *Journal of Law & Contemporary Problems*. After that he went to Paris where he worked at UNESCO for the improvement of cultural relations and progress in human rights, and studied the emerging Absurd theatre. Returning to the States after Joe McCarthy but not "McCarthyism" was finished, he began to write absurdist plays of his own.

The Swings had its premiere at Gene Frankel's Weekend Repertory Theatre in New York, was also performed at the Arena Stage in Washington, and published in *Evergreen Review*. *Borgeois Gentleman* and *Hoo Fasa* had staged readings at the Washington Theatre Club. *Myrtilus* (with music by Dina Kosten) and *The Americans* were performed at Ellen Stewart's La Mama Experimental Theatre in New York.

After de Grazia met Barney Rosset, the legendary founder of Grove Press, the two worked together to free from censorship the Grove editions of William Burrough's *Naked Lunch*, the Swedish film *I Am Curious — Yellow*, and Henry Miller's *Tropic of Cancer* (in the U.S. Supreme Court). During the Vietnam War he was associated with the Institute for Policy Studies, served as a lawyer for the Mobilization to End the War in Vietnam and was an organizer of Volunteer Lawyers to Defend the Demonstrators at the Pentagon.

De Grazia is a member of the founding faculty of the Cardozo Law School (Yeshiva University) in Greenwich Village where he continues to teach and write about, among other subjects, the freedom and censorship of literature, art, and film in America. He is the author of a history of the struggle for artistic freedom in the United States called *Girls Lean Back Everywhere: The Law of Obscenity and the Assault on Genius* (Random House and Vintage).

CHARACTERS

WIFE

CHILDREN, A DAUGHTER AND SON

HUSBAND

THE NEIGHBOR'S WIFE

THE APPLIANCES

SCENE: *The living-dining area of a cheap two-bedroom brick bunga-low in a development forty minutes from a metropolis. There is a great "picture-window" which looks out upon a row of identical cheap two-bedroom brick bungalows with identical great "picture-windows" looking out upon identical . . . etc., etc. Within the win-dows may be seen pantomine scenes identical to that which takes place on the stage. The furnishings are American "Colonial;" they clash with the modern dress of the husband and his wife. On the wall, a crocheted portrait of the American flag, and other oddities. The place is in dreadful taste, but the couple raising their family there are trying.*

There is a giant-size TV screen in constant operation, its im-age visible, even oppressive, to the audience. The volume is at max-imum, probably in an effort to overcome the terrible, ear-splitting and brain-deadening sounds coming from THE AIR CONDITIONER, THE AUTOMATIC DISHWASHER, THE AUTOMATIC WASHER-DRYER COMBINATION, THE AUTOMATIC DISPOSAL, THE RE-FRIGERATOR-FREEZER, *and* THE TANK-TYPE VACUUM CLEANER, *which interminably grind, humm, swish, tumble, buzz, bang, shift gears, roar, gurgle and groan—obscuring the human sounds that the characters seek, from time to time, to make. In fact, their sweet docility is best accounted for by their final submission to the aural vitality of these mechanical helpmate devices.*

As the scene opens, the TV image is delivering a late-afternoon "soap-opera", the heroine of which is an aging, once-beautiful mother whose marriage is going on the rocks, whose teenage son has just been arrested for smoking marijuana in high school, whose beloved father is dying of cancer, and who has suddenly grown aware that she is fast becoming, if not already there, an alcoholic, etc. The sound from the TV, when it surfaces above the raging ocean of sounds coming from the other appliances, is apparently out of sync. Worse yet, as gradually becomes evident, the dialogue is from another "soap-opera" — D.H. Lawrence's Lady Chatterley's Lover.

When the CHILDREN enter, the TV image will deliver animated cartoons, with a soundtrack composed of readings from the book Auschwitz or Letters From Vietnam, or another.

When the HUSBAND enters, the TV image will deliver the news and weather of the day with soundtrack running smart personal commercials for ladies, à la Vogue, Glamour, etc. He will be very tall and thin, with a mustache; neatly dressed in a gray flannel suit, etc. The WIFE will enter with a rush, from the Kitchen [O.S.]. She will wear ballet slippers, tapered slacks, a frilly tea-apron, a ladies-model man's shirt, no make-up, and hair-curlers under a kerchief. A cigarette will dangle from her lip. She will wear her ANXIETY mask, as from an impossible number of household chores to be done by an impending deadline. The living-dining room, however, appears immaculate.

The WIFE enters, and all the APPLIANCE sounds come on. She moves to THE VACUUM CLEANER, takes its neck or handle, in her hand, doesn't switch on the power, stands and looks at the TV screen. Her body, rigid at first, relaxes slowly. She goes rigid once more, then relaxes, still watching the TV. As the reading from Lady Chatterley's Lover becomes recognizable, she turns on the power but does not push the machine. THE VACUUM CLEANER'S sound grows and subsides, huskily, having a life of its own. As the READING becomes a bit tense, the WIFE's body also grows tense, and THE VACUUM CLEANER has an orgasm in the WIFE's hand. The WIFE's body sort of sags. THE VACUUM CLEANER'S sound subsides. The other mechanical sounds grow remote and smooth out.

The CHILDREN enter the house. They are twins, boy and girl, aged 5. They carry schoolbooks underarm. When they enter, they stand impassively at the threshold.

The WIFE springs to life, cuts off THE VACUUM CLEANER, darts to and around the CHILDREN, and all around the room. Her mask of ANXIETY flickers with lights of JOY. She returns to her original position, facing them at the door, lays her hand upon THE VACUUM CLEANER handle or neck, and speaks.

WIFE: [*Singing.*] Watch what you are doing!

> Don't make a mess of things!

> Where have you been all day?

> Go to your room and play!

[*The* CHILDREN *remain immobile. The boy, however, makes a faint move with his hand or mouth, as though he wishes to speak; This propels her once more into agitated motion, around the room, around them, and back again as before.*]

WIFE: [*Singing.*] Do you want something to eat?

[*The* CHILDREN *lick their lips and she springs OS into the kitchen.*]

WIFE: [*OS*] [*Singing.*] All right! I'm coming! All right!

> All right! All right! All right!

> I'm coming! All right!

> [*Enters with cookie jar.*] All right!

[WIFE *stuffs cookie after cookie into their mouths, boy, girl, boy, girl, etc. They swallow as fast as they can. She gets an extra cookie into the boy when the girl's swallowing falls behind...*]

WIFE: [*Singing.*] All right! All right! I'm coming! All right!

> [*pause*] All...right....

[WIFE *watches them swallow the last cookies and, as their faces suffuse with dumb contentment, her mask changes from* ANXIETY *to* JOY.]

[*The* CHILDREN *shake the crumbs from their hands and continue to smile contentedly. The* WIFE *leaps and dances around them and the room, joyfully, returning to her first position.*]

WIFE: [*Singing.*] All right!

> Then watch! But I have so many things to do.

> Please stay out of my way!

> Here!

[*She takes them up by their coat collars, as a cat her kittens, and deposits each on a hook of a coat rack standing in a corner of the room.*

They dangle there, their smiles of contentment marred a bit by the helplessness of their situations.]

[WIFE *returns to her* VACUUM CLEANER, *switches it back on; it and the other household sounds mount once more to a raging ocean of sound.*]

WIFE: [*Sings.*] Busy day!

> Busy day!
>
> Every one is such a busy day!
>
> Busy day!
>
> Busy day!
>
> Every one is just a busy day . . .

[WIFE *slows ("runs") down to immobility, looking at the TV screen. THE VACUUM CLEANER'S sounds subsides too; but all the other sounds of the APPLIANCES grow in power and variety and run rampant through the room. A LONG TIME passes.*]

[*The light outside the "picture-window" fades.*]

[*The door opens again.*]

[*The HUSBAND enters carrying a briefcase and a mask of* FATIGUE. WIFE *springs to life. The other mechanical sounds subside to buzzes and a hum.* THE VACUUM CLEANER *returns to life with a welcoming roar and a new surge of power, which drown out the words* HUSBAND *has to say upon entering.*]

[WIFE *darts to him, pecks his cheek, closes the door, darts around the room, back to him, pecks his other cheek, takes his briefcase,* EXITS *with it into bedroom, enters without it, darts to bar, makes* GIANT MARTINI, *darts with it to him, takes his nose in her fingertips, opens his mouth, pours* GIANT MARTINI *into him, watches him swallow and go glassy-eyed. She looks at him lovingly.*]

WIFE: [*Sings.*] Darling, you can use a drink.

> When you come home from work.
>
> You can always use a drink.

[WIFE *returns to bar, makes another* GIANT MARTINI, *returns to him, feeds him it in the same manner as before, watches lovingly as he turns even more glassy-eyed than before.*]

WIFE: [*Sings.*] There! There!

> There!
>
> That's better, dear?
>
> Isn't it? Better, dear?
>
> There! There?
>
> There!

[WIFE *studies him, remembers something, moves up to him, loosens his tie, unbuttons his shirt collar, removes his hat, smooths down his hair, caresses his shoulder, singing:*]

> There...?
>
> There...?
>
> There...?

[WIFE *rubs against him.*]

HUSBAND: [*Responding.*] Unng!

WIFE: There...? [*Pause.*] Stop! [*She looks around the room.*]

> Not before the children... Don't forget our children! Think about... the children [*Looking around, unable to locate the children.*]

HUSBAND: UNGHHhhh...

WIFE: Besides! Wouldn't you like another...?

[*She goes swiftly to bar, pours another GIANT MARTINI, returns, feeds it to him in the same manner as before.*]

> There!

HUSBAND: [*Wobbling, caving, straightening, caving.*] Enhhhh......

WIFE: [*Helping him to sofa.*]

> Hard day. You've had a hard day.
>
> All work and no play means
>
> Dad-dy's had another hard day.

WIFE: [*Cont'd.*] [*She sits him down on the sofa, he caves, she sits him up, he caves, she props him up with pillows.*]

It's all right! All right! It's all right!

There!

[WIFE *looks around, spies the* CHILDREN *who are staring at them, dashes to them.*]

[*Singing.*] All right? Is everything all right?

[*She darts out and returns with more cookies.*]

[*Singing.*] If you'd rather not go and play in your room

You may stay and watch......

[WIFE *stuffs more cookies into their mouths.*]

But please don't spoil your appetite!

[WIFE *goes to the* HUSBAND, *takes* GIANT MARTINI *glass from him, smiles.*]

You mustn't spoil your appetite either!

[WIFE *exits with glass, returns to* VACUUM CLEANER, *begins to sweep.* THE VACUUM CLEANER *and all the other* APPLIANCES *roar back to life.*]

WIFE: [*Singing madly above the turbulent ocean of sound.*]

Happy day! Happy day!

Every one is such a happy day!

Happy day!

Happy day!

Every one is just . . . a happy . . . day . . .

[*The* WIFE *slows ("runs") down, into immobility.* THE VACUUM CLEANER *subsides. The other* APPLIANCES *rock and roll victoriously about the room.*]

[*The* NEIGHBOR'S WIFE *enters.*]

[*The* WIFE *snaps back to life, darts to her, then around the room, leaving* THE VACUUM CLEANER *standing, dusting all the furniture, the walls, doors, etc. then returning to original position.*]

WIFE: Won't you come in!?

Come in!

How very nice to see you.

You're almost like a stranger.

Come in! Won't you come in!

It's been so very long. Let's see...

N.W.: [*Drily.*] Before lunch. I dropped in before lunch.

WIFE: Let me see...

N.W.: To borrow some sugar. We talked 'til...

WIFE: Let me see...

N.W.: ...o'clock. Three or four. O'clock.

WIFE: How could it have been three... or four o'clock. You're mixing up today with yesterday... o'clock. O'clock.

N.W.: [*Drily.*] Yesterday, I dropped in after breakfast.

To try out your electric blender.

We talked 'til five or six... [*Looking around.*]

That was yesterday.

WIFE: [*Flitting around room, dusting, etc.*] Ha! ha!

Oh dear! Ha! ha! Well...

N.W.: Whenever I drop in

We talk 'til three or four.

Or five

Or six... [*Looking around.*] o'clock... o'clock.

WIFE: What?

N.W.: O'clock. What would my husband say?

WIFE: What?

N.W.: Yes. What would your husband say? O'clock.

WIFE: I wonder.

N.W.: I wonder, too.

WIFE: I wonder.

N.W.: I wonder... too.

> too... O'clock.
>
> Too... [*She stares at the* HUSBAND, *glassy-eyed on the couch.*] *o'clock!*

WIFE: [*Following her eyes.*]

> What in the world did you drop in at this time for, Nicole? It's
>
> so
>
> very... late...

N.W.: [*Staring at* HUSBAND.]

> I know.

WIFE: You know how much I love to stop

> And hear you talk.
>
> You shouldn't stay too long,... Nicole?

N.W.: [*Staring at* HUSBAND.]

> I know.

WIFE: This time. O'clock.

N.W.: [*As before.*] I know.

WIFE: Please don't misunderstand my meaning...

N.W.: [*Turning to go, seeing the children, pop-eyed on the coat-rack.*]

> No. O'clock.

WIFE: They're so dear to me. I want to be prepared.

N.W.: [*Staring at the children.*] The children... the children...

WIFE: And don't forget my husband. He'll be home too, soon. He'll... be home... soon, too. O'clock. I have to be prepared. [*She starts* THE VACUUM CLEANER *and the other* APPLIANCES *begin also to come on.*]

WIFE: [*Cont'd.*] The children come first

        But my husband comes, too.

        You see?

        Don't you see?

        I want to be prepared.

        [*Stopping abruptly.*] [*Leaving the* APPLIANCES *on.*]

        I wonder where they can be?!

        They're home so late from school.

        Maybe they're outside playing.

        Should I go out and see ...? [*Putting on a scarf.*]

        Excuse me? Excuse me! [*Exiting.*] But I'd better

        go out and see ...

N.W.: [*Staring at the closed door, looking around the room. listening to the appliances, noticing* THE VACUUM CLEANER.]

        [*To audience.*] She must be crazy! [*Moving to sofa.*] O'clock.

        [*Sitting down beside* HUSBAND *who, as before, smiles glassy-eyed at all and nothing.*]

        HELLO.

        I think your wife must be crazy. O'clock. O'clock.

        Running out on you this way. O'clock.

        I think your wife must be crazy...

        Hello... [*He doesn't change countenance: she seizes his shoulders and kisses his lips, passionately.*]

        I know how long you've been waiting to do that, to me

        How long. Too long. I saw how you were watching me ... so long.

        Through my window. For so long. [*Pause.*]

N.W.: [*Cont'd.*] She can't satisfy you, can she? [*Seizing and kissing him again, more passionately.*]

You're not like all the other men, here, around here.

N.W.: [*Cont'd.*] All the other men around here...aren't men at all.

They all look exactly the same, no matter what's their name.

Horn-rimmed glasses and a gray-flannel suit.

Smiley-mouth and glassy-eyed, too.

You're...different! [*She kisses him again and removes his coat and shirt.*] [THE VACUUM CLEANER *revs up and the D.H. Lawrence reading begins to repeat.*]

What's different about you is...brains... [*Kisses him.*]

I like a man who can...think and see... [*She unbuckles his belt and starts to remove his trousers.*] [THE VACUUM CLEANER *is running amuck.*]

I like a man...who's a MAN... [*She pulls down his trousers so that he sits wearing only underwear and shoes and gartered socks.*]

[*The* CHILDREN'*s eyes pop out unbelievingly*]

With a big DICK...for me...oh! [*She has found his tiny dick.*]

[THE VACUUM CLEANER *subsides with an uncharacteristic whistle, but the other* APPLIANCES *run and grind and whirl and tumble and gyrate and scream raucously, as the* WIFE *enters.*]

WIFE: Dear, oh dear! Dear, oh dear!

Where in the world can the children be?!

[*Spotting children.*] Oh!

[*Rushing to them, kissing their faces.*]

There you both are! I almost forgot!

N.W.: [*Swiftly re-making her face: new lipstick, powder, eyebrow pencil, mascara.*] Excuse me . . . Excuse me . . . I didn't look . . .

I didn't . . . see.

WIFE: How you were!

What love was all about!

[*She hugs them lovingly and the* CHILDREN *start to scream, hideously, piteously, as if all the horror which they have seen was only now felt. Their screams encourage even more heroic efforts from the* APPLIANCES, *and* THE VACUUM CLEANER *starts to huff and puff.*]

[*The* NEIGHBOR'S WIFE *rises from the sofa, straightens her clothes, straightens up the* HUSBAND *on the sofa, kicking his outer clothes underneath and starts to leave.*]

N.W.: So nice to see you!

Too bad. Too bad.

Maybe they are hungry.!

I think he could use some sleep. [*Exits.*]

Too bad. I'll drop in again soon. Too bad.

I'll be seeing you . . . soon . . .

WIFE: [*Taking the* CHILDREN *down from their hooks, carrying them OS into a bedroom.*]

Don't cry, my darlings!

Brave children don't cry

Please don't cry my darlings

Tomorrow brings a brighter day....

[*The* APPLIANCES *quiet down. The* HUSBAND *remains as before, seated in his underwear, glassy-eyed, his face now smeared with red. There is a long silence. Then the* WIFE *enters, very slowly, stops, looks at her* HUSBAND.]

WIFE: Hello.

I almost didn't see . . . you.

Hello.

[*The* HUSBAND *topples over onto the floor.*]

WIFE: You've been drinking again, haven't you.

> Oh Tom, you've been drinking so much again,
>
> Haven't you!

WIFE: [Cont'd.] Trying to unwind.

> We know you're only trying to unwind ... but ...

[*She takes him by the feet and draws him gently OS from the room.*]

WIFE: Silly day.

> Silly day
>
> Every day is just a silly day.
>
> Silly day.
>
> Silly ... day ...

Christopher Durang

MRS. SORKEN

Mrs. Sorken by Christopher Durang. Copyright © 1997 by Christopher Durang. All rights reserved. Reprinted by permission of Helen Merrill, Ltd.

CAUTION: Professionals and amateurs are hereby warned that *Mrs. Sorken* by Christopher Durang is fully protected under the copyright laws of the United States of America, the British Commonwealth, including the Dominion of Canada, and other countries of the International Copyright Union and Universal Copyright Convention, and are subject to royalty. All rights, including professional, amateur, motion picture, recitation, lecturing, public reading, radio and television broadcasting, and the rights of translation into foreign languages are strictly reserved. Particular emphasis is laid on the question of readings, permission for which must be secured from the author's agent in writing.

All amateur and professional stage performance rights (other than first class rights) to *Mrs. Sorken* are controlled exclusively by Dramatists Play Service, 440 Park Avenue South, New York, NY 10016. No professional or non-professional performance of the play may be given without obtaining in advance the written permission of Dramatists Play Service, and paying the requisite fee. Inquiries concerning all other rights to *Mrs. Sorken* should be addressed to the author's agent, Helen Merrill, Ltd., 435 West 23rd Street, Suite 1A, New York, NY 10011, USA.

Christopher Durang

Christopher Durang has had plays on and off-Broadway including *The Nature and Purpose of the Universe, Titanic, A History of the American Film, Baby with the Bathwater, Beyond Therapy, Laughing Wild,* and *Sex and Longing.*

His play *Sister Mary Ignatius Explains it All for You* won Obie Awards for him and actress Elizabeth Franz when it originated at Ensemble Studio Theatre. A subsequent production by Playwrights Horizons on a double bill with his *The Actor's Nightmare* transferred to Off-Broadway, where it ran for two years. *Sister Mary* has had productions around the country and the world.

His play *The Marriage of Bette and Boo* also won him an Obie Award, as well as the Dramatists Guild's prestigious Hull Warriner Award, when it premiered at the New York Shakespeare Festival. Durang also played the part of Matt in that production, sharing with the other nine actors an Ensemble Acting Obie Award. The play's director, Jerry Zaks, and designer, Loren Sherman, also won Obie Awards for their work on that play.

Among his most recent work was *Durang Durang*, an evening of six one-acts directed by Walter Bobbie at Manhattan Theatre Club. Included in this evening were *Mrs. Sorken, For Whom the Southern Belle Tolls* and *A Stye of the Eye.*

Mr. Durang has also acted in movies, such as *Housesitter, The Butcher's Wife,* and *Mr. North.* He sang in the Sondheim revue *Putting it Together*, which starred Julie Andrews at the Manhattan Theatre Club. He also performed with Sigourney Weaver in their co-authored cabaret, *Das Lusitania Songspiel*; and with John Augustine and Sherry Anderson in the *Chris Durang and Dawne* cabaret.

Durang is a graduate of Yale School of Drama; a member of the Dramatists Guild Council; and with Marsha Norman is the co-chair of the playwriting program at the Juilliard School Drama Division.

CHARACTERS

MRS. SORKEN

Enter Mrs. Sorken to address the audience. She is a charming woman, well-dressed and gracious, though a little scattered. She is happy to be there.

MRS. SORKEN: Dear theatregoers, welcome, and how lovely to see you. I've come here to talk to you about theatre, and why we all leave our homes to come see it, assuming we have. But you have left your homes, and you're here. So, welcome!

Now I have written down some comments about theatre for you, if I can just find them.

[*Searches through her purse.*] Isn't it refreshing to see someone with a purse?

[*Looks some more through the purse.*] Well, I can't find my notes, so I'll have to make my comments from memory.

[*From here on, she is genuinely winging it — some of it may be thoughts she prepared, much of it is thoughts that pop into her head as she is speaking. She is not nervous, though. She loves talking to the audience.*]

Drama. Let's begin with etymology, shall we? ... etymology, which is the history of the word.

The word "drama" comes from the Greek word "dran," which means to do, and which connects with the English word "drain," meaning to exhaust one totally, and with the modern pharmaceutical sedating tablet, Dramamine, which is the trade-name of a drug used to relieve airsickness and seasickness and a general sense of nausea, or *nausée* as Jean-Paul Sartre might say, perhaps over a cup of espresso at a Paris bistro. How I love Paris in the spring, or would, if I had ever been there; but Mr. Sorken and I haven't done much traveling. Maybe after he dies I'll go somewhere.

We go to the drama seeking the metaphorical Dramamine that will cure us of our nausea of life.

Of course, sometimes we become nauseated by the drama itself, and then we are sorry we went, especially if it uses the F-word and lasts over four hours. I don't mind a leisurely play, but by 10:30 I want to leave the theatre and go to sleep. Frequently,

I prefer Dramamine to drama, and only wish someone would renew my prescription for Seconal.

Secondly...we have the word "theatre," which is derived from the Greek word "theasthai," which means to view.

And nowadays we have the word, "reastat," a device by which we can dim the lights in one's house slowly, rather than just snapping them off with a simple switch.

And thirdly, we have the Greek god "Dionysus," the last syllable of which is spelled "s-u-s" in English, but "s-o-s" in Greek, the letters which in Morse code spell "help" — "Dionysos" is the god of wine and revelry, but also the father of modern drama as we know it.

The Greeks went to the theatre in the open air, just like the late and wonderful Joseph Papp used to make us see Shakespeare. Shakespeare's language is terribly difficult to understand for us of the modern age, but how much easier when there's a cool breeze and it's for free. If it's hot and I have to pay, well, then I don't much like Shakespeare. I'm sorry, I shouldn't say that. He's a brilliant writer, and I look forward to seeing all 750 of his plays. Although perhaps not in this lifetime.

But back to the Greeks. They went to the open-air theatre expecting the drama they saw to evoke terror and pity.

Nowadays we have enough terror and pity in our own lives, and so rather than going to the theatre looking for terror, we go looking for slight irritation. And rather than looking for the theatre to evoke pity, we look merely for a generalized sense of identification as in "Evita was a woman, I am a woman." Or "Sweeney Todd was a barber, I go to the hairdresser." Or "Fosca in *Passion* should have her moles removed, I know a good dermatologist." That sort of thing.

But did the Greeks really experience terror and pity? And if so, what was it in all that matricide-patricide that so affected them?

I know that seeing Greek drama nowadays, even with Diana Rigg in it, really rather baffles me, it is so very different from my own life. My life with Mr. Sorken is not something that Diana Rigg would wish to star in, even on PBS. My life, I'm sorry to say, is not all that interesting.

Indeed, addressing you at this very moment, I'm sorry to say, is the high point of my life to date.

Could I have lived my life differently? Women of my generation were encouraged to marry and to play the piano, and I have done both those things. Is there a piano here? I don't see one. I might have played a sonata for you, or a polonaise.

But back to my theme—Drama, from the Greek word "dran."

When we leave the drama, we return to our homes feeling "drained." And if it's been a good night in the theatre, we leave feeling slightly irritated; and feeling identification with Evita or Fosca or that poor Mormon woman in *Angels in America*.

And so, drained, we get into our nightgowns, we adjust our reastats from light to darkness, we climb into bed next to Mr. Sorken, we fall into a deep REM sleep, dreaming God knows what mysterious messages from our teeming unconscious; and then in the morning we open our eyes to the light of the new day, of the burgeoning possibilities.

Light from the Greek word "leukos," meaning white, and the Latin word "lumen" meaning illumination. In German, *der Licht*; in French, *la lumière*. All art leads to light.

Light. Plants need light to grow. Might people need art to grow? It's possible. Are people less important than plants? Some of them are certainly less interesting.

But there is some connection between theatre and light, and people and plants, that I am striving to articulate. It's about photosynthesis, I think, which is the ingestion of light that plants go through in order to achieve growth.

And you see, it's "light" again — "photo" comes from the Greek word, "phos," which means light and which relates to phosphoresence, or the "light given off." And synthesis comes from the Greek prefix,"syn-" meaning together, and the Greek word "tithenai," meaning to place, to put.

Photosynthesis — to put it together with light.

We go to the theatre, desperate for help in photosynthesis.

The text of the play is the light, the actors help put it together, and we are the plants in the audience.

Plants, lights, theatre, art. I feel this sense of sudden interconnection with everything that's making me feel dizzy. Dramamine, of course, is good for dizziness.

Now to wrap up.

Dear theatregoers. I hope you enjoy your evening this evening. I'm not quite sure what you're seeing, but whatever it is, I'm sure it will be splendid.

And, by the way, if you are ever in Connecticut, I hope you will drop in and say hello to me and Mr. Sorken. He prefers that you call first, but I love to be surprised. So just ring the bell, and we'll have cocktails.

And I hope you have enjoyed my humbly offered comments on the drama. I have definitely enjoyed speaking with you, and have a sneaking suspicion that in the future, it is going to be harder and harder to shut me up.

[*Either end with that, or possibly add and end with: "And so, the high point of my life to date being over, I leave you with the play."*]

Gus Edwards

FOUR WALLS

Four Walls by Gus Edwards. Copyright © 1997 by Gus Edwards. All rights reserved. Reprinted by permission of the author.

CAUTION: Professionals and amateurs are hereby warned that *Four Walls* by Gus Edwards is subject to a royalty. It is fully protected under the copyright laws of the United States of America, and of all countries covered by the International Copyright Union (including the Dominion of Canada and the rest of the British Commonwealth), and of all countries covered by the Pan-American Convention and the Universal Copyright Convention, and of all countries with which the United States has reciprocal copyright relations. All rights, including professional, amateur, motion picture, recitation, lecturing, public reading, radio broadcasting, television, video or sound taping, all other forms of mechanical or electronic reproduction, such as information storage and retrieval systems and photocopying, and the rights of translation into foreign languages, are strictly reserved. Particular emphasis is placed upon the question of readings., permission for which must be secured from the author's agent in writing.

All inquiries should be addressed to Applause Books, Licensing Division, 1841 Broadway, Suite 1100, New York, NY 10023. No amateur or stock performance or reading of the play may be given without obtaining, in advance, the written permission of Applause Books.

Gus Edwards

Gus Edwards was born in the Caribbean, but studied theatre in the U.S., where he worked as an actor. Mr. Edwards is the author of thirteen full length plays produced by the Negro Ensemble Company (NEC) and other places. Titles include *The Offering*, *Weep Not for Me*, *Lifetimes on the Streets*, and most recently, the single-character play *Confessional*. He has also written for PBS-TV.

Edwards, who has received grants from the Rockefeller Foundation, National Endowment and the Arizona Commission for the Arts, currently teaches Theatre and Film Studies at Arizona State University, where he also runs the Multi Ethinic Theatre Program.

Publications by Gus Edwards include *Old Phantoms* and *The Offering* (Dramatists Play Service), *Three Fallen Angels*, (Centerstage Anthology), *100 Monologues* (Mentor Books), *Classic Plays from the NEC* (Univerisity of Pittsburg Press) and Monologues on Black Life (Heinemann Books).

Four Walls was originally presented by the Writers Circle and the Actors Theatre of Phoenix at the Herberger Theatre (Stage West) on August 1, 1996 with the following cast: Ellen Benton as Rose, Ken Love as Ralph and Lillie Richardson as Judy. It was directed by Glorianne Engel.

This play is dedicated to Glorianne Engel and the Writers Circle.

CHARACTERS

RALPH   A man in his twenties.

ROSE   His wife — late forties

JUDY   An attractive but tough looking girl between 18 and 23.

SETTING: *Despite the title, a room without walls. Sort of a lighted area surrounded by a void of darkness. Furniture should be kept at a minimum. A sofa, two chairs, and something that represents a replica of an old statue. It doesn't have to be very elaborate — just suggestive.*

TIME: *The present.*

SCENE 1

Night. Late. ROSE *is sitting alone in the room doing needlepoint. Music from a radio can be heard softly in the background. The feeling is lonely, even bleak.* ROSE *remains in her chair for a while quietly doing her work. Outside the room a dim light illuminates* JUDY *and* RALPH.

RALPH: Take just about a minute. Don't move.

JUDY: You sure?

RALPH: Told you, I'll handle it.

JUDY: Ralph —

RALPH: Baby —

JUDY: Okay man. It's your scene. [*He kisses her.*]

RALPH: Be right back.
     [*He moves into the room as the lights fade on* JUDY.]

ROSE: Ralph?

RALPH: Hey Rose, I didn't think you'd still be up.

ROSE: I was just going in.

RALPH: Oh, yeah . . . Kinda late for you ain't it?

ROSE: I was doing, some stuff . . . You hungry?

RALPH: No . . . No thanks. Er—

ROSE: I have food all prepared. Sure you don't want something?

RALPH: No. I ate already. Downtown you know.

ROSE: Oh.

RALPH: Yeah, it was getting late, I was getting hungry so—

ROSE: Alright.

RALPH: But, thanks anyway.

ROSE: Sure.

RALPH: Listen—er—Rose.

ROSE: Yes?

RALPH: I got a favor to ask you.

ROSE: Uh-huh?

RALPH: And if it ain't okay, you tell me.

ROSE: Sure. What is it?

RALPH: Well , you see , I ain't exactly alone.

ROSE: Oh.

RALPH: I have a friend with me. Somebody I met—well—tonight.

ROSE: A woman?

RALPH: No not a woman. A child. Couldn't be no more than—Oh I don't know. A child anyhow. I met her wandering around the streets. No place to go. Talking about sleeping in the subway, on a night like this. So—I told her she could stay the night. Here on the sofa. That's if it is okay with you.

ROSE: Yes. It's all right.

RALPH: Look—you don't have to say so if it ain't.

ROSE: I know.

RALPH: I mean this is your place too. We—both live here.

ROSE: I know.

RALPH: So if it ain't okay —

ROSE: But it is, Ralph.

RALPH: You sure?

ROSE: I told you before, yes.

RALPH: Alright.

ROSE: Where is she?

RALPH: Outside. One minute. I'll get her.
     [*He exits.* ROSE, *almost as a reflex, begins straightening up things in the room. After she's finished, she pauses for a moment staring off into space. Her appearance and manner gives the impression of great weariness. Moments later* RALPH *returns with* JUDY.]

RALPH: [*Cont'd.*] Honey, this is Judy — the person I was telling you about. Judy, this is my wife Rose.

JUDY: Hi.

ROSE: How do you do?

JUDY: Oh — I'm fine. How are you?

ROSE: I'm fine too. Thank you.

RALPH: Hey, hey, everybody's fine. Well that's nice. Real nice.

ROSE: Yes.

JUDY: Uh-huh.

ROSE: Have a seat, won't you.

RALPH: Yeah, sit down. Rest your bones. I was just telling Rose how I met you.

JUDY: Oh. Yeah — I was hanging out, with no place to go, then I met Ralph.

ROSE: Are you new to the city?

JUDY: Nooo. Well — kinda new, I guess. Came in from Detroit. I been living with this guy couple a months now. And, well, we had this fight. Dumb stuff. Everything will probably be okay tomorrow when I see him. But tonight I'm kinda stuck. No money — and no place to go.

ROSE: Don't you have any family or friends?

JUDY: Oh I know a couple of people, but I'm kind of embarrassed to go knocking on their door at this hour. I'd rather sleep in the subway.

RALPH: But you don't have to. At least not tonight anyway.

JUDY: Yeah. Thanks. You're really kind.

ROSE: Thank Ralph. He's the kind one.

RALPH: You're in it too, honey.

ROSE: Yes. I guess.

JUDY: Well, thanks to both of you.

RALPH: Hey, the least we can do is give somebody a helping hand from time to time. Ain't that so baby?

ROSE: Yes.

RALPH: I mean if we don't look out for each other, who gon do it. Right?

ROSE: Right

RALPH: Black folks got to stick together and that's a fact.

JUDY: Right.

RALPH: Absolutely.

> [*There's a pause in the conversation as everybody tries to think of something to say.* JUDY, *looking around the room, begins to take interest in the statue.*]

JUDY: That thing is nice. Real nice. Where'd you get it?

RALPH: Rose made it. Down in the cellar. She makes all kinds of things. That's how she makes her living.

JUDY: Yeah?

ROSE: Uh-huh.

RALPH: When somebody wants a copy of some famous statue or sculpture all they have to do is order it and Rose goes to work.

ROSE: My father was a sculptor, so I took up his profession. Only,

FOSE: [*Cont'd.*] he could make beautiful, original things. Me, I just have a talent for reproduction.

JUDY: Well, I don't know what to say except I think they're really, really good.

ROSE: Thank you . . . that's nice to hear. [*She rises.*] It's getting late. I guess we better prepare some place for you to sleep.

JUDY: Look, I don't want to put you to any trouble.

ROSE: No trouble. No trouble at all. I'll get some pillows. [*She goes off.*]

JUDY: Ralph —

RALPH: It's okay.
[ROSE *returns.*]

ROSE: Here you are. The bathroom's over there. I'll get you some clean towels.

JUDY: I wish you wouldn't go to —

ROSE: Don't worry about it.
[ROSE *gives her the towels.*]

JUDY: Thank you.

ROSE: I forgot to ask. Have you eaten?

JUDY: Yes, that's how I spent the last money I had.

ROSE: Can I get you anything?

JUDY: No, thanks.

RALPH: We got beer in the box. You want a beer?

JUDY: Well, if somebody else is having one.

RALPH: Rose?

ROSE: No, I don't think so.

RALPH: Come on honey, break down.

ROSE: No. Not tonight. I'm tired.

RALPH: Suit yourself. Well, it's just you and me, Judy. Two beers, coming right up. [*He goes to get them.*]

ROSE: You're an attractive young woman.

JUDY: Thank you.

ROSE: But you should take better care of yourself. You look a little — tired.

JUDY: I been up a long time.

ROSE: It shows.
[RALPH *returns.*]

RALPH: Here you go. [*He gives* JUDY *a beer.*] Sure you don't want one, Rose?

ROSE: No. It's late. I'm turning in.

RALPH: Oh, alright. Let me just finish this. I'll be right behind.

ROSE: Take your time. Goodnight, Miss —

JUDY: Judy.

ROSE: Judy.

JUDY: Goodnight Rose. Thank you.

ROSE: Thank Ralph. [*To* RALPH.] Goodnight.

RALPH: See you in a while, baby.
[*ROSE exits. JUDY and RALPH stand there looking at each other.*]

JUDY: Ralph I —

RALPH: Shhhh — [*Indicating* ROSE *in the bedroom.*]
He goes over to the radio and turns it up a bit, but not too loud. Then returns to Judy who's staring out of the window.

RALPH: It's a quiet night out there. And cold.

JUDY: [*Sensing him but not looking back.*] Ralph, I don't know.

RALPH: But in here it's cozy.

JUDY: Ralph —

RALPH: Don't talk. Turn around. Look at me.
[*He kisses her lightly, then draws her more firmly to him, kissing her more strongly.*]

JUDY: Ralph, I don't know.

RALPH: Baby, why you have to talk? There's only you and me, baby. Just you and me. And the long night ahead of us.

[*They kiss again. Somewhere in back we see* ROSE *not looking at them, but present almost as a witness to their coupling. She makes the sign of the cross and begins to pray.*
Lights fade to black.]

SCENE TWO

Morning.
    RALPH *enters partially dressed carrying a leather jacket.*

RALPH: Rose. . . Rose?

ROSE (OS): Yes.

RALPH: Listen baby. I need some money.
    [*While he's waiting,* RALPH *puts on the jacket and inspects it in the mirror.* ROSE *enters.*]

RALPH: [*Cont'd.*] What do you think, baby? Real leather. Bought it off a guy on the street. Sixty bucks.

ROSE: It looks nice.

RALPH: I'm talking about the fit. In back.

ROSE: It fits fine. Looks good on you.

RALPH: Smells good too. Here, take a whiff. English leather. You can't beat the price.

ROSE: Was it hot?

RALPH: Of course. That's the only time you get a bargain in this city. But, you got to know what to buy. There's a lot of junk out there. But this was a good deal. A real good deal. [*Admires himself some more in the mirror.*] You know, that's what you ought to do. Get yourself some new clothes and things.

ROSE: Why?

RALPH: Make you feel good.

ROSE: But I feel good already.

RALPH: I mean happy — inside.

ROSE: I feel happy.

RALPH: You sure? Because sometimes I look at you and you look like the loneliest woman in town.

ROSE: I'm not lonely.

RALPH: You sure?

ROSE: Yes. I have you, don't I?

RALPH: Course, you do. And don't you ever doubt it. [*He holds her close to him.*]

ROSE: I won't. . . . Ralph.

RALPH: Hmmmm?

ROSE: That girl, did she leave?

RALPH: Yes.

ROSE: Is she coming back?

RALPH: No. She asked me to say good-bye. And to thank you.

ROSE: I'm not the one she should thank.

RALPH: Well, she thank you anyway.

ROSE: That was nice of her.

RALPH: You didn't mind her spending the night, did you?

ROSE: No.

RALPH: You're really great. You understand me so.

ROSE: I love you, Ralph.

RALPH: I know. And I love you too baby.

ROSE: Yes . . . How much do you need.

RALPH: Ohh — I think about twenty'll do.

ROSE: Here.

RALPH: Thanks. [ROSE *gets her shawl.*] You going out?

ROSE: I'm going to church.

RALPH: Yeah? You been doing that more and more.

ROSE: It makes me feel good. Inside.

RALPH: Well, that's where it counts, I suppose.

ROSE: Yes.

RALPH: Look, I probably won't be here when you get back. I'll see you later tonight.

ROSE: Alright. I'll cook something for you to eat.

RALPH: You don't have to.

ROSE: I know.

RALPH: I'll see you later then, baby. Have a good day.
[*She leaves.* RALPH *goes back to the mirror and finishes dressing as the lights fade*]

SCENE THREE

Night. Late. The same as in Scene One.
    ROSE *rises, puts away her stuff, turns off the radio and the lights, then goes in. Moments pass. Suddenly there's a desperate pushing on the buzzer, followed by a frantic knocking on the door.*

RALPH (OS): Rose! Rose! Wake up, baby! Hurry! Wake up, please. Hurry!

ROSE: [*Returning.*] Ralph?

RALPH (OS): Rose! Rose, open up.
[*She rushes off stage to him.*]

ROSE (OS): Oh my God! My God! Ralph — what happened?

RALPH: [*Stumbling in.*] Help me honey . . . Help me! [*He's clutching his stomach, his shirt is quite bloody.*]

ROSE: [*Hand over her mouth.*] Ralph —

RALPH: I'm hurting baby. Hurting bad . . . I got cut. Some guys up the street jumped me. They wanted my money . . . I gave it to them, but they cut me anyway.

ROSE: Oh Jesus, Ralph . . . Jesus. [*She begins to cry.*]

RALPH: Don't cry baby . . . Don't cry. I'm hurt and bleeding. Bleeding real bad . . . You got to help me.

ROSE: Yes. Yes, of course.

RALPH: You got to go get me to a doctor . . . Call emergency or something.

ROSE: Yes . . . I will, I will. But — first we got to get you warm. And comfortable. You're shivering. You look cold.

RALPH: I am cold . . . Rose!
[*She goes for a blanket.*]

ROSE: [*Returning.*] I'm here. Not going anywhere. I'm right here. [*She puts the blanket around him.*] Now doesn't that feel better?

RALPH: Yes . . . yes it does. But you got to move baby. You got to call a doctor . . . Or an ambulance. This thing is bad. I can feel it.

ROSE: Yes darling, yes. I will. I will . . . Now put your head on this pillow. Rest softly.

RALPH: Honey, I mean it. I'm bleeding to death . . . I—I ain't joking . . . this is for real. I'm bleeding and my guts is falling out.

ROSE: I know.

RALPH: Then for God's sake Rose, do something! Call somebody, hurry.

ROSE: Okay. Just rest and relax. All will be fine.

RALPH: Honey . . . Honey, you saying that, but you ain't moving.

ROSE: Just lie still. It'll be easier if you don't move so much.

RALPH: Easier? What are you talking about? Call the man. I'm about to pass out.

ROSE: Rest easy, baby. Lie still.

RALPH: Honey —

ROSE: Relax —

RALPH: But Babe —

ROSE: Please Ralph. Don't move.

RALPH: Don't —? [*He tries to rise.*] Why?

ROSE: It's alright, honey. I'm here. Here to make it easy for you.

RALPH: What you talking about? Make what easy? Baby, you okay?

[*He rises, makes two steps toward the phone, then falls.*] Rose, please help me. Call somebody.

ROSE: Can't. The phone's been broke for a week.

RALPH: [*Shouting with his last strength.*] Well gooddamnit then. Do something! Go outside, get a cab . . . [*A plea.*] Do something.

ROSE: I can't leave you alone like this. Not now. Not when you need me.

RALPH: Baby, baby — you ain't understanding. I'm hurt and bleeding. I'm dying and I can feel it. My life is just —

ROSE: I love you Ralph. Love you very much.

RALPH: Honey, please —

ROSE: From the first time we met I loved you. And, as time went on, I loved you more.

RALPH: Oh God — Jesus — somebody, Help me!

ROSE: They said you were too young for me. And that I could never hold you — but I did, didn't I? You may have strayed but you never left.

RALPH: [*A cry of pain.*] Rose!

ROSE: Hold unto me, baby. Just hold unto me. I'm right here.

RALPH: Honey — baby . . . I'm cold.

ROSE: [*Rocking him.*] Sleep . . . Sleep baby . . . sleep.

RALPH: [*Pulling away from her.*] You . . . you want me to die. [*A sudden realization.*] That's what it is. You ain't doing nothing because . . . because — you want me to die. You glad this is happening to me. You happy! You — you — Oh my God — you hate me!

ROSE: I love you, Ralph.

RALPH: You — been hating me — all this time.

ROSE: I been loving you — loving you all this time.

RALPH: Well, if you do, help me. Call the police.

ROSE: No.

RALPH: I — don't understand you. I — ain't following —

ROSE: Because this is the end, Ralph. The end — here with me.

RALPH: No — no it can't be. [*Shouting.*] SOMEBODY PLEASE, HELP ME!

ROSE: [*Calmly.*] You've had a good life. A rich life. Roof over your head, clothes, money, love . . . and all the women you could get. You've had a lot, Ralph. A whole lot. And now it's all over. This is the end — here with me.

RALPH: Oh Jesus — Jesus. You gone nutty baby. Talking this strange . . . weird talk . . . Oh God . . . you gone crazy . . . burying things in the yard, being by yourself all the time . . . It messed you up . . . it's this place . . . This goddamn place. Staring at these four walls. It done something to you . . . and all that church going. You been praying on me — praying for something bad — Oh God . . . Jesus — I don't want to die. I don't want to —

ROSE: Ralph . . . Ralph, don't worry. Everything will be the same. I love you baby. I love you, and always will. There'll never be anybody else. Ever. You hear. Every year on your birthday I'll put flowers in your room. I'll light candles in church and say prayers. You'll have a nice funeral. Flowers, organ music, everything. I'll shine your shoes myself. And you'll wear your new suit and gold cuff links . . . There'll be a Cadillac, a long shiny black one to drive you on your way . . . And there'll be more, lots more . . . Nothing's too good for the man I love.

[*She rises, goes to the phone and dials.*]

ROSE: [*Cont'd.*] Yes I want to report an emergency . . . My husband has just died in my arms. Yes . . . yes, I'll be right here waiting. Thank you. [*She returns to the sofa where* RALPH *is still lying.*] There now it's all taken care of. Everything is going to be just fine.

[ROSE *then sits with his head on her lap. After a while she begins to rock him and hum as the lights fade.*]

THE END

Herb Gardner

I'M WITH YA, DUKE

I'm With Ya, Duke by Herb Gardner. Copyright © 1997 by Herb Gardner. All rights reserved. Reprinted by permission of the author.

CAUTION: Professionals and amateurs are hereby warned that *I'm With Ya, Duke* by Herb Gardner is subject to a royalty. It is fully protected under the copyright laws of the United States of America, and of all countries covered by the International Copyright Union (including the Dominion of Canada and the rest of the British Commonwealth), and of all countries covered by the Pan-American Convention and the Universal Copyright Convention, and of all countries with which the United States has reciprocal copyright relations. All rights, including professional, amateur, motion picture, recitation, lecturing, public reading, radio broadcasting, television, video or sound taping, all other forms of mechanical or electronic reproduction, such as information storage and retrieval systems and photocopying, and the rights of translation into foreign languages, are strictly reserved. Particular emphasis is placed upon the question of readings, permission for which must be secured from the author's agent in writing.

All inquiries should be addressed to Marion Philips, 411 East 53rd Street, New York NY 10022, (212) 355-3716.

Herb Gardner

Herb Gardner is the author of *A Thousand Clowns*, *The Goodbye People*, *Thieves*, *I'm Not Rappaport* (which won the 1986 Tony Award for Best Play, the Outer Critics Circle Award for Outstanding Play, and the John Gassner Playwriting Award), and *Conversations With My Father*. His one-act plays include *How I Crossed the Street for the First Time All by Myself*, *The Forever Game*, and *I'm With Ya, Duke*. For his film adaptation of *A Thousand Clowns*, Gardner won the Best Screenplay Award from the Screenwriters Guild as well as Academy Award nominations for Best Screenplay and Best Picture of the Year. He also wrote the screenplays for *Thieves*, *The Goodbye People* (which he also directed), and *Who Is Harry Kellerman and Why Is He Saying Those Terrible Things About Me?* — this last being an adaptation of one of his several short stories, which appeared in *The Best American Short Stories of 1968*. In addition, Mr. Gardner is the author of a novel, *A Piece of the Action*. He is currently adapting his award-winning play *I'm Not Rappaport* for the screen.

CHARACTERS

SAMUEL MARGOLIS

DR. ALBERT MACINTYRE

NURSE'S VOICE

RED BARBER'S VOICE

SCENE: *A semi-private room in a brand new wing of St. Mary's Hospital in Brooklyn; 1975. A hanging rod and curtain separate the two beds. One is unoccupied, the mattress folded, and can be seen through the pulled-back curtains.*

In the other bed, asleep, is SAMUEL MARGOLIS; *late seventies, several days' growth of beard, wearing a baseball cap with "Dodgers '55" printed on it. He is attached to a heart-monitoring machine by two slim tubes to his chest, a travelling line on the screen indicates heart and pulse beats, which are regular. An I.V. tube is attached to his left arm: to the Right of the bed is an intercom button and speaker, a table with a phone and a manuscript. This is* SAM's *will. A television set is mounted high and at the Center of the wall opposite the bed, to the Right, a simple wooden cross. On the right wall a somber but tasteful painting of the crucifixion.*

AT RISE: *It is 8:30 at night and the darkened Brooklyn skyline is seen through the large window at Left.* SAM *is asleep. We hear the regular hum and blip of the heart-monitor machine.*

SAM: [*Murmuring.*] Yessir. Yessir. All fresh today. Strawberries. Beauties. Do yourself a favor. The bananas, forget it. I don't personally recommend...

[*He opens his eyes, squinting.*] What the hell is this? What's going on here?

[*He looks about, sees crucifix.*] Oh boy... oh boy... Terrific.

[*Sees the I.V. on his arm and the two tubes for the heart-monitor.*] One thing sure... I'm not visiting here.

[*He sits upright.*] Okay. What's up? What's cookin' here? What's doin'?

[*Punches intercom button.*] Hello somebody! This is Margolis! Speak to me!

NURSE'S VOICE: [*On intercom.*] Yes, Mr. Margolis.

SAM: Who I got here?

NURSE'S VOICE: This is Nurse Carswell.

SAM: O.K. What am I doin' here? Where am I?

NURSE'S VOICE: Mr. Margolis, every night at this time you ask me the same —

SAM: I'm not looking for hot news. Answer me again, I wouldn't be bored.

NURSE'S VOICE: Mr. Margolis, you are on the eighth floor of St. Mary's Hospital in Crown Heights. It is Tuesday night, eight p.m...

SAM: Perfect...

NURSE'S VOICE: You have suffered a coronary occlusion...

SAM: Expensive...

NURSE'S VOICE: You were brought here under emergency circumstances...

SAM: Five, six hundred dollars...

NURSE'S VOICE: and have been here exactly one week.

SAM: Fifteen hundred dollars, easy. I gotta get outta here, one more week they'll name a pavilion after me. A week? A week I'm here.
     [*To intercom.*] Yes, I knew it was a week. Of course, a week. I knew that.
     [*To himself.*] A week. Wow...who's watching the fruit store? Shimkin, the thief. A whole week now. There won't be an orange left.
     [*To intercom.*] Who brought me here?

NURSE'S VOICE: Your son.

SAM: Which one? I got one in Europe, finding himself. One in Los Angeles, a lawyer puts you to sleep on the telephone, and the Dopey. The Dopey put me here, right? Jack. Jack the Dopey. Look where he put me. Of course, only Jack.
     [*His hand to his heart.*] I remember now...I was in the store...Bingo...

SAM: [*Cont'd.*] [*Into intercom.*] You' re the Night Nurse, *Cars*well ...
I remember now ...

NURSE'S VOICE: Yes, sir.

SAM: [*Leaning toward intercom.*] Listen, it wouldn't hurt you could
lose a couple pounds. [*He looks at the empty bed.*] Ortega.
Where's Ortega? I was just talking to Ortega ...

NURSE'S VOICE: Oh, I thought you knew ... Mr. Ortega ... Mr.
Ortega expired early this afternoon.

SAM: Expired? What was he, a driver's license? [*Quietly.*] Dead.
Ortega. He died. Well, that'll teach me, you can't make friends
in a place like this. Talked to me all night. Told me his whole
life. That's what people do, Carswell. Something tells them
they're dying and they hand it over, the inventory ...

NURSE'S VOICE: Mr. Margolis. Your surgeon, Dr. MacIntyre, will
be visting you shortly to discuss the operation tomorrow —

SAM: Save him a trip. I'm not doing it. I lost interest. That's enough
living. That's it. [*Turns off intercom. Dialing phone, singing very
softly.*] "Who stole my heart away ... who ..." [*Into phone.*]
Hello, Dopey. Let me tell you about my will; you're not in it.
How come you put me here? ... I don't care emergency; look
where I am! How could this be a hospital? It don't have the
word "Sinai" in it. Listen, Dopey. No operation. The release
form. I'm not signing. No signing. No operating. I'm seventy-
eight-and-a-half. It's enough. Love to the children. [*Hangs up.*].
[DR. ALBERT MACINTYRE *is standing in the doorway. Late 30's, a
tasteful suit with a vest and a near smile that has carried him
through many rooms and many conversations like these.*]

DR. MACINTYRE: Mr. Margolis ...

SAM: What?

DR. MACINTYRE: Hello, I'm Dr. Albert MacIntyre ...

SAM: [*Correcting him.*] No, you're his son, you're Dr. MacIntyre's
son! What is it, a child surgeon? How old are you?

MACINTYRE: I'm thirty-seven.

SAM: Come back when you're fifty-two; we'll talk business.

MACINTYRE: I've been asked by your internist to look in on you... [*Sits on chair next to bed.*] Dr. Cramer and I both feel that I should describe to you the purpose and necessity of tomorrow morning's surgery... The purpose is, of course, to prolong life. In your case, I would safely say, by several years. Life in relative physical comfort, with a minimum chance of future attack. We have located an obstruction in the anterior descending branch of the coronary system. That part of the heart, which this artery supplies, is being deprived of blood and oxygen. Now, what we'll be doing tomorrow, Mr. Margolis, is inserting a bypass, a small new channel for the blood to get through, a supplementary vessel that will be —

SAM: Speaking of boats, Al, I came to this country on a boat, the Princess Mara, me and Benny Kalsheim; April the Seventeenth, Nineteen Seventeen, three and a half years older than the century. A lot of people aren't informed but half the boats went to New Orleans which is where I was. Came to New York later, up the river like Jazz from the South. We went, me and Benny, first to Tompkins Corners in South Carolina. They made me the sheriff there. Could you believe it? Sheriff Margolis! The only English I knew was "Hello" and "What's goin' on here?" In my wallet there, a picture of me, the Sheriff. I had a uniform and a star and dreams you wouldn't believe. A fruit store was not on the horizon. Benny is still there, he stayed and I came to New York City. Why am I telling you this? You should know me. You should know whose heart you're talking. [*A small moment of fear.*] Or maybe I'm just doing what Ortega did with me yesterday...

MACINTYRE: Of course. Well then... [*Takes out a Xeroxed drawing of a heart and a pencil from vest pocket.*] Mr. Margolis, let me sketch for you, roughly, what we'll be doing tomorrow morning... [*Sketching briskly on the heart-drawing.*] Now, the operation is designed to improve the circulation of blood through this area of the heart muscle... [*Pencil slips from his hand and falls to the floor.*] Oh, I...

SAM: [*Cups his hands around his mouth, shouting to the room in general.*] Cancelled ! Operation cancelled ! Forget it ! Unavailable ! Not

SAM: [*Cont'd.*] even considering at this time! [*Punches intercom button.*] Nurse! Nurse! There's a kid in here plays with knives! He'll hurt somebody. Get him outta here !

MACINTYRE: That's amusing, the pencil . . .

SAM: Listen, there's a call for you. I hear them calling you . . . in the hall . . .

MACINTYRE: Mr. Margolis, we —

SAM: [*Quietly, genuinely.*] Listen, Al . . . The fact is I'm putting you on altogether . . . I got no intentions for this operation. I'm not doing it anyway. I just been stringing you along; you're a busy fella, goodnight.

MACINTYRE: Is there something about the operation that . . .

SAM: No, it's a cute operation. I'm saving the picture.

MACINTYRE: What is it that you object to?

SAM: Living. It's time to go. I'm not interested no more.

MACINTYRE: Is there some particular reason that you —

SAM: Look out the window. I'll show you.

MACINTYRE: Mr. Margolis —

SAM: Al, go look . . .

[*MacIntyre goes to the window.*]

SAM: [*Cont'd.*] That's it. You see what they're doin'? Whatever they're doin', I don't want to be party to it no more. The times, these times, ain't my time. They took too much away without a snappy notion what to put instead. When I was sherriff there was still dreams for things. They don't do that no more; cash and carry and what's for supper. I personally knew this a long time, and last week my heart found out. You see the cap? Brooklyn Dodgers of Fifty-five. I do them honor.
   [*Sitting at edge of bed.*] Nobody came to take their place . . . They took Ebbets Field away. You take the pyramids away from Egypt all you got is sand and rotten weather. Walter O'Malley, he sells them like shoes without even discussing. What's left? Banks! You don't got *teams* now, MacDonald, you got Marine

SAM: [*Cont'd.*] Midland plays Chase Manhattan! The heart went with them and Brooklyn started to die. What's to root for? Without what's to root the voice goes away. Duke Snider! He went away! A lifetime in the afternoon hollering "I'm with ya, Duke, I'm with ya," never dreaming for a moment that he wasn't with me. Edwin Donald Snider, six feet tall, a hundred and eighty pounds, bats left, throws right, lifetime average Two Ninety-Five — a person you *knew*, went to Los Angeles, which doesn't even exist. They threw the lions to the Christians. They all went. The names, just say the names, you could sing them: Amoros, Gilliam, Campanella, Furillo, Hodges, Padres, gone, even the sound is gone...What's left? A cap. I got a cap. Dodgers Fifty-five, and sometimes I hear in the summer, on the wind, Red Barber's voice... [*Leans toward the Doctor; quietly.*] It's a sign of the whole thing. Time got my heart, the Dopey's got my name, and Shimkin the Thief got my fruit store by now. What was, isn't. What could be, didn't happen. Altogether: check-out time for Margolis!

MACINTYRE: Mr. Margolis —

SAM: Forget it —

MACINTYRE: If you would —

SAM: Listen, they had an expression for this in the old country: [*Shouting.*] "Get outta here!"

MACINTYRE: Certainly, Mr. Margolis. I am not particularly attracted to your abuse. And any further time spent listening to your farewell address does not interest me. [*He rises.*] You will not enjoy dying, Mr. Margolis. Without this operation another coronary occlusion will be fatal, and this attack could occur at any hour, perhaps tomorrow, the next day; next week. But make no mistake; you are killing yourself. It won't be the world, or Walter O'Malley, and certainly not me. I've been listening to you; I thought you were at least angry enough to live. [*Silence for a moment.*] Am I mistaken? Answer me, Mr. Margolis.

SAM: [*Silent for a moment, then he points to the Crucifixion painting.*] It's a hospital; they couldn't put somebody in better shape on the wall?

MACINTYRE: Good evening, Mr. Margolis. [*Goes to door.*] I can't say that it's been a pleasure.

[*He exits.* SAM *sits, frustrated, pulls his cap down sharply, brooding for a moment.*]

SAM: [*Suddenly shouting.*] Hey you! Macintosh! Hey, Al!

[MACINTYRE *has been standing just outside the doorway. He steps back in.*]

MACINTYRE: Yes...

SAM: O.K. I'll give you a break.

MACINTYRE: You changed your mind. Why?

[*No response.*]

MACINTYRE: [*Cont'd.*] Why?

SAM: [*After a moment.*] Curiosity !

MACINTYRE: You'll have to sign the release paper.

SAM: Yeah. O.K. [*He writes something on the paper, then signs it, looks up.*] You're a drinker? You drink a little?

MACINTYRE: Only while I'm operating. [*Looks at release paper.*] You wrote something here...

SAM: I added a clause to the contract.

MACINTYRE: "C.O.D "?

SAM: Yeah, you deliver me back in the shape I gave you: that is, living; and then you get paid. On delivery.

[MACINTYRE *smiles.*]

SAM: [*Cont'd.*] Look, I could die from this operation, right?

MACINTYRE: There is that possibility. Not a strong one, but a possibility.

SAM: O. K. I'll see you tomorrow.

MACINTYRE: Fine.

SAM: No parties...

MACINTYRE: O.K. [*Going out the door.*] Good night.

SAM: [*Shouting.*] Hey, Butterfingers!

MACINTYRE: Yes . . .

SAM: [*Quietly; a genuine threat.*] You kill me and I'll make your life miserable . . . I'll haunt you, Sweetheart; you understand? I'll haunt your closet and your suits'll make you crazy.

MACINTYRE: Good night . . .

SAM: [*As* MACINTYRE *goes out the door.*] Good night! Go home and go to sleep!

> [SAM *alone in the empty room. A moment of fear, of weakness, of exhaustion. He quickly picks up phone, dials. Speaks into phone: brightening, his energy returning . . .*] Hello, Dopey? Here's the latest on the will; you're still not in it. They say I could be dead tomorrow so here's last wishes. Instruct my lawyer, Klein, all money goes to Benny Kalsheim, Tompkins Corners, South Carolina. Tell him it's from the Sheriff. Call Shimkin, tell him whatever he's doing he'll never get away with it. Tell your daughter Jennifer, start the guitar lessons again; music is a good thing. Tell your mother the Doctor says absolutely her cooking did it. Meanwhile, if I don't see you again, goodbye and good luck.

[*He hangs up; enormously satisfied by this burst of energy. He closes his eyes. We begin to hear the sound of* RED BARBER'S VOICE, *barely audible at first and then building very gradually as it fills the room. The sound of cheering fans builds with the excitement of his familiar voice.*]

BARBER'S VOICE: . . . the pitch to Lavagetto, swung on and missed. Fast ball, it was in there, strike one. Gionfriddo walks off Second, Miksis off First, they're both ready to go at anything; two men out, last of the Ninth. The pitch — swung on, there's a drive out toward the Right Field corner, Henrick is going back, he can't get it, it's off the wall for a base hit . . . here comes the tying run . . . and here comes . . . the winning run . . .

[*Barber's voice is lost in the sound of the cheering crowd as*

THE CURTAIN FALLS.]

Susan Hansell

MY MEDEA

My Medea by Susan Hansell. Copyright © 1997 by All rights reserved. Reprinted by permission of the author.

CAUTION: Professionals and amateurs are hereby warned that *My Medea* by Susan Hansell is subject to a royalty. It is fully protected under the copyright laws of the United States of America, and of all countries covered by the International Copyright Union (including the Dominion of Canada and the rest of the British Commonwealth), and of all countries covered by the Pan-American Convention and the Universal Copyright Convention, and of all countries with which the United States has reciprocal copyright relations. All rights, including professional, amateur, motion picture, recitation, lecturing, public reading, radio broadcasting, television, video or sound taping, all other forms of mechanical or electronic reproduction, such as information storage and retrieval systems and photocopying, and the rights of translation into foreign languages, are strictly reserved. Particular emphasis is placed upon the question of readings, permission for which must be secured from the author's agent in writing.

All inquiries concerning professional, stock, and amateur rights should be addressed to Applause Books, Licensing Division, 1841 Broadway, Suite 1100, New York, NY 10023. No amateur or stock performance or reading of the play may be given without obtaining, in advance, the written permission of Applause Books.

Susan Hansell

Susan Hansell is a native of California. She graduated from Berkeley with high honors in 1981. Plays of hers which were produced on the west coast in the 1980s include *Pink Rope*, *A Day In*, and *14 Ladies in Hats*. A commissioned work, *American Rose: Our Gals on the Homefront, 1941-1945* premiered in 1997 at the Ohio Theatre in New York City. Her new plays are *Rollover Othello* (nominated for a Pushcart Prize as published in *Oasis* Jul-Sep 1996), *Queen of Sheeba*, *Romance with Jana*, and *Quicksilver, Quicksand*. *My Medea* was first published in *Oasis* Oct-Dec 1996. Ms. Hansell has had poems, essays and dramatic texts published in magazines and anthologies, including Heinemann Press's 1996 *More Monologues by Women for Women*. She resides in Brooklyn, New York, where she is employed as an adjunct lecturer in the CUNY system.

CHARACTERS

HOUSE BOY
CHAUFFEUR
M.J. MEDEA
CHORUS OF LOS ANGELES MEN
TWO POLICEMEN
MRS. MEDEA
BEST FRIEND OF M.J.
THREE ATTORNEYS
THE MEDIA
A STREET PREACHER

Also, in non-speaking roles:
MRS. MEDEA'S MOTORCYCLE ENTOURAGE

SETTING: *A wealthy Los Angeles subdivision, in front of the Medea mansion, as represented by scaffolding or like structures which allows view of the interior.*

HOUSE BOY: [*Entering from the house.*]

God I wish man never launched jets across the skies,

　　Flying through blue, or cut stadiums or cities

　　From the earth's blood. If only men weren't men at all,

　　And black and white weren't colors; then My Man wouldn't

　　Be hot like some thermo-nuclear thing, with his

　　Head in a melt-down, just thinking about this wife.

We worship M.J. Medea in this country.

　　What reason is there for a wife to leave The Man.

　　Now there's hatred in every suburb, and love looks

　　Like trash. She refuses him, and he calls on the

　　Public to witness her vacancy sign. In the

　　Motel of stars, NO is no answer for M.J.

HOUSE BOY: [*Cont'd.*] When night falls, he feeds his global ap
  petites.

  With white lines and love from the ladies. Left alone,

  He throws his head back and shouts out for his mother,

  And for the family he left when he married such

  A chick. My Man, wanted mucho by the whole world,

  Has discovered the suffering of any lame guy.

M.J. Medea won't tolerate such treatment.

  Why should he? Celebrities have toxic tempers;

  Plus, the stuff of my dumb life is too low to

  Be touching him. The situation is tense, man.

  If he unnerves, he could quake us all down. Check it out.

  I'm too young and good-looking to grieve. Got that?

CHAUFFEUR: [*Entering.*] Why are you standing outside talking to
  yourself?

  Mr. M.J. wants you inside, to watch the house.

HOUSE BOY: Listen, old man, if you were truly good help you'd

  Feel for the boss when his luck ran out. Have a heart.

  I've worked myself into a full-on anxiety attack.

  I had to come outside and tell my troubles

  To the green, green lawn here, and to the spacious air.

CHAUFFEUR: The man's mood is still poisonous, day and night.

HOUSE BOY: Still. Are you kidding? It's the BEGINNING of it.

CHAUFFEUR: Oh well — not that it matters what I know or do

  But we oughta be worried about what's coming—

HOUSE BOY: What are you saying? Do you know something? Spill
  it.

CHAUFFEUR: Nothing. Forget it. Nothing to be done.

HOUSE BOY: Hey, we work together. You can't keep things from
    me.
    Fair is fair. [*Pause.*] Do you think I'm a gossip or what?
CHAUFFEUR: Alright, alright. I heard some people, who will go
    Unnamed, talking the other day, in the garage
    Where I get the Rolls serviced. According to those
    In the know, Mrs. Medea plans to stick it
    To M.J. permanently. The Missus. is fed
    Up with the fans he lets see him, suck him, and shake
    His hand. He ain't easy to talk to, neither, she
    Says; says he leaves her alone, nine nights out of ten.
    So she won't take him back; he's like any Common
    Joe. She's got a regular lawyer, and she split
    With his kids. A come-down for us all, eh? No good. [*Pause.*]
    That's what I heard anyway. But what do I know.
HOUSE BOY: No good. Are you crazy? This is the worst possible
    Thing. How could Our Man deprive his public of...
    What's she thinking? She can't think one woman'd be
    Enough for him. Impossible. Insulting. [*Pause.*] Can the
    Missus. take the children from him? I don't believe it.
CHAUFFEUR: Out with the old and in with the new. [*Pause.*] Yet
    I doubt Mrs. M. knows just what's going on around here.
HOUSE BOY: I'm starting to hate her. It's her fault these clouds
    Above us are so hard. It looks like sixty nights worth.
CHAUFFEUR: Well you didn't hear it from me. And keep your flap
    Shut. He's mad enough without hearing news from us.
HOUSE BOY: Can you believe their mess. I wish she were dead.
    No I don't. Understand. She's a nice lady —
CHAUFFEUR: Are you that young? People seem nice, but love can

CHAUFFEUR: [*Cont'd.*] Hurt like hell. No one knows what goes on

behind closed

Doors. Besides, we only love ourselves when pushed.

HOUSE BOY: Maybe I have a lot to learn. It's weird, but like,

I don't wanna be in that house with him. He cuts

His eyes at anyone who happens by. One minute

He's hot; the next, he's cold. Somehow his cold is

Worse than his hot—

CHAUFFEUR: —Earthquake weather, my mother said.

Mrs. M. oughta know better'n to piss him

Off. I know I sure won't be anywhere around.

[*CHAUFFEUR exits, muttering.*]

M.J. MEDEA: [*As seen within the house, pacing etc.*]

I won't take this. No. NO. I WON'T.

This won't happen. Not to me. NOOOOOO —

I was created. To have my

Way. MY WAY. I. Am. MEDEA.

HOUSE BOY: Oh no. What did I tell you. Is that bad or what.

M.J.: No. No. No. NO WOMAN tells me

How it's gonna be. People love

Me. ME. I'm The Man here, goddamnit.

That's the way it is. Shit. No

Woman leaves me. Never. NEVER.

It can't happen here. It won't. NO.

Who does the bitch think she is. Shit.

She'll burn before I fall. MOTHER.

NO NO NO NO NO NO NO NO.

HOUSE BOY: It's true. Our heroes aren't admired for their

Moderation. No, humble mediocrity

HOUSE BOY: [*Cont'd.*] Never inspired a goddamned thing. The flip side

Is, everyone's afraid to contradict him.

And here's how the man-made-gods get by with their murders,

While the rest of us chickens sweat it out. Watch.

CHORUS OF LOS ANGELES MEN: [*Entering, the* CHORUS *members speak their sentences/sentence groups/ sentence fragments as both individuals and as groups or choral sub-groups, which may correspond to a specific choreographed pattern.*]

I heard the voice, I heard the yells

Of Our Wretched Idol, M.J.

Our father in heaven, he raves;

Across the valley, on the shore,

From the freeways that divide our

Homes; I heard his shouts, I heard

His moans. I'm sorry for The Man;

We're all outraged for this...loss. No

Woman can get away with chip,

Chipping away at his Holy

Marble. [*Pause.*] Hey, you there, house boy. What's

The latest word on Medea?

HOUSE BOY: Americans bury the bodies of mortals.

You cheer for the good guys with the horses-n-guns.

What can winning at such games mean to the Medea.

Which peons will be torched in his bitter grip.

CHORUS: What? Talk English, man. And speak up!

M.J.: [*From within.*] Death is better than this defeat.

I'll wipe-out the whole town for this

HUMILIATION. I want rain,

M.J.: [*Cont'd.*] Mud-slides, fires and riots. AAAAARRRRRHHH.

She'll pay for this. THE WHORE. Somehow.

CHORUS: Jesus Christ. Did you hear that shit.

We can't let her bring him down. And

We can't let him start wishing

For death-n-destruction. He could

Make it happen. This is M.J.

We're talking about. Yeah. The Man

Can do whatever he wants. Yeah.

Let bygones be bygones is the refuge

Of chumps. Everyone deserves

What they get in the end. Listen.

M.J.: She will NOT cripple me. NO SLUT

Will show me up. [*Laughs.*] Your Barbarian!

I was the outcast who soared

To the top. I'm The Man of all

Men. Now I call the shots. No woman's

All that. I'll teach her a damned

Lesson she'll be sorry about.

For the city to see, for men

To hear: She'll find out what's up.

HOUSE BOY: Do you hear how he's talking, and the threats he
makes.

On our Lady of Guadalupe, virgin of

Faith and necessities, I'll pray for roses. But

Only a crown of thorns will satisfy his thirst.

CHORUS: [*Chiming in.*] It's our time to aid and comfort

M.J. The Man needs his fans. Yeah.

He's my friend, and I'm willing to

CHORUS: [*Cont'd.*] Help, no matter what. We're on his
    Side. Yeah. What other side is there?
    Shit, man, no one can touch HIM. That's
    The way it is. Yeah. [*To* HOUSE BOY.] Why don't you
    Go in and tell him we're outside. [*Pause.*]
    Hurry up, boy. Now he needs us.
    His wrath isn't chump change. Move it.
HOUSE BOY: OK, OK. But I doubt if it'll do squat.
    Whenever I approach . . . well, if looks could kill
    You'd have to find someone else to order around . . .
    [*Pause.*] Did you ever think about how stupid
    Your pop music is? Your favorite songs yak all day
    About love and how great it is. Why don't you have
    Songs about betrayal and disappointment. [*Pause.*] I'm going.
    But I think the radio should play songs that help
    People deal with how things really are.
    Either that, or songs shouldn't have words at all. Sounds
    Alone can't fool, or be taken away to dust.
        [*HOUSE BOY exits into the house.*]
CHORUS: I hear M.J.'s cries against the
    Woman who wronged him. Betrayal
    Of love is an abyss
    Unlimited as the sea.
    M.J., over us, does not merit this hit.
        [M.J. *enters from the house.*]
M.J.: Men of Los Angeles. I have come outside to
    Show you a thing or two. Our situation is
    About to improve. I know. Life isn't easy

M.J.: [*Cont'd.*] For the average man. Don't think I've forgotten

My roots. I haven't. A guy has to make money

Just to get a woman, and if you marry her,

She wants more. Yet it's worse to be without one.

There's no escape. And you never know if you'll take

A good or a bad one. So once married, a dude

Has to be a mind reader to understand the

Creature in his bed. If she's a saint, then life's great.

If she's a whore, then your whole world's better off dead.

She takes your money and goes shopping. She's happy.

A man goes out every day into the desert

Of the streets. He's a refugee; he's a warrior.

He sees the worst that life offers. The only thing that

Keeps him going is knowing his woman is at

Home, behind him, no matter what, always. You know

What I mean. In the end, a guy needs his heroes;

Men need to be fans of a MAN BEYOND their own

Meagerness: To give glory to an image of

MAN UNBOUND by work a day worlds. After

The oil change, after monogamy and the

Orthodontist, you're owed your sweet fantasies. My

Medea will live on for you, conquering the women

You can't touch, as master of cities you'll never

Visit. For your dreams, it's my duty to strike out

Any mortal who seeks to destroy your source.

I ask only this from you, that my way of pay-back,

My plan of vengeance, will be honored among us.

CHORUS: Yes, I promise. And I swear.

CHORUS: [*Cont'd.*] You're right. It's fitting to

> Maintain the order. Common
>
> Men are crippled enough. True.
>
> But our Medea... NO. Yeah,
>
> It's a stinking landfill of
>
> A town we live in. No, none
>
> Of us should put up with it.
>
> Look how she treated him. Yeah.
>
> Pictures in the *National*
>
> *Enquirer.* Shaking her
>
> Stuff up and down Rodeo Drive.
>
> Shit. She had everything she
>
> Could want. And still she wasn't
>
> Satisfied. Typical broad.
>
> Yeah. Of course we're angry. Of course
>
> HE'S angry. Of course you're angry!

M.J.: In all ways, a man must be like steel, strong and

> Uncomplaining. But when his beliefs are wronged, a man
>
> Must hold thoughts of blood. Come, hear my mighty-fine
> plan.

CHORUS: Wait up. Two of L.A.'s finest.

> What do they want? What's up with this?

TWO POLICEMEN: [*Entering, they alternate lines, with one cop domi-
nating and speaking most of the longer lines, while the second cop
punctuates the first's, speaking most of the short lines/words.*]

> Mr. M.J. Medea? Of course, we know who
>
> You are. Right. We hate to bring you bad news. Our job
>
> Is never easy. Try to understand. We have
>
> To follow orders. That's the way it is, you see.

M.J.: I hope nothing's wrong, officers. What could be, uh?

POLICEMEN: It's none of our business. Of course not. The facts can't

Be right. They're exaggerated. No doubt. But still . . . .

M.J.: Spit it out guys. I can take it. What's the problem?

POLICEMEN: Right. This isn't easy. Sure, I know how women

Can be. But it seems that your ex has filed a

Complaint against you. Right. She says you entered her

House, broke a few things and slapped her around a bit.

A misunderstanding, huh? Right. She mentions some

Prior incidents. Marriage is no picnic, that's

For sure. Looks like she's taking legal action to

Keep you away from her and your kids. That's too bad.

See this complaint form? It comes with a warrant. We

Should take you downtown with us. Right. Just to talk . . .

M.J.: Guys, guys, is that really necessary? Come on.

Now whatever's going on with the woman, this

Here's between the men. You know how they can change things

Around. Before you know it, they've got it all fixed

Against ya. If she's having a bad-hair-day, look

Out. Don't mention it if you ran into one of her

Friends at the Beverly Center. You'll be fast

Accused of spousal abuse, or worse. A guy can't win.

This complaint, and the warrant? Impossible, uh?

Female imagination gone crazy. I say,

The crime is my children are hers, and my wife's out

With her Hollywood crowd, in the vehicles I

Bought with my bucks. I have to go downtown with you?

POLICEMEN: Of course we sympathize with you. I'm on your side,
   Mr. Medea. We all know how wives can be.
   But it looks like yours is serious here. You've got
   To prepare yourself for a fight. Allegations
   Like these won't die of their own accord. If your ex
   Persists, she can drag you in front of the judge, and
   Then there won't be a thing we boys-in-blue can do
   For you. Right. That's the way it is. If she wants
   To make trouble, well, I hope for your sake she don't.

M.J.: So what happens now, with today's little problem?

POLICEMEN: Tell us about the events she cites. Are they true?

M.J.: It hurts me to know you would consider them so.

POLICEMEN: I have to ask, sir; it's my job. I don't like it.

M.J.: Of course, of course. How insensitive of me, boys.

POLICEMEN: If we'd found you not at home...It's possible...

M.J.: M.J.? He's out in Malibu now. No problema.

POLICEMEN: I guess we can keep this visit between us men.

M.J.: What visit? [*Laughter.*] Do you want a drink before you go?

POLICEMEN: How about an autograph, Mr. Medea?

M.J.: Sure, sure. And call me M.J., boys. Anything else?

POLICEMEN: I think you better steer clear of your ex-wife, sir.

M.J.: What do you mean? I haven't seen the bitch in weeks.

POLICEMEN: Right, right. Then this complaint is really not true.
   Wow.

M.J.: I told you, the bitch lies. I don't want to see her.

POLICEMEN: It's for your own good; for the court, and custody.

M.J.: Of course, of course. I'm just kidding you. Is that it?

POLICEMEN: Right. We'll be going. But don't forget, we weren't
   here.

[*All laugh.*]

M.J.: And since I wasn't either, I won't say good-bye.

[M.J. *salutes sarcastically;* POLICEMEN *salute back, then exit.*]

CHORUS OF L.A. MEN: What a bitch. What a travesty.

'S up with those cops, man. Without their

Blue suits they'd have no huevos to

Ask the time. And forget about

Telling M.J. what to do. Like

They're doin' him a favor. I

Don't think so. Nope. Nothin' but

A homeboy when push comes to shove.

M.J.: Down, boys. Don't worry about it. I don't need your

Sympathy. Everything's under my command. I've

Got the plan. It's normal for the boys-in-blue to

Take a swing at the big block. Don't sweat it; I'm up

To the challenge. Inside, I'm still the kid from your

No-where-lands. You all know my pavement-to-the-

Paradise-of-Los Angeles story. You know how.

The Beautiful People love a kid who fights for

Their gold. Don't think I've gotten FAT. Look at me, uh?

I remember Oak-town. I remember myself;

The kid who out-ran, out-spit, and out-thought all of

God's children. And I was Enough to know what to

Do with it. I became your sportsworld gladiator,

Your dollarbill hero, your global-trade-magnet, and

Your biggest hero of intercourse idol-making ever, uh?

Now, this bitty pestilent female trouble,

A test of my manhood and brains? HA.

I know precisely what to do. She's dead meat.

CHORUS: Right. For sure. He's in control.
    He's making sense. Go M.J.
    Ride, man. Dude, we're with ya.
    Yeah. You know it. No high-horse
    Answers to the judge of the
    Foot-men. We have no choice.
    But M.J.? He's too high to die.

M.J.: I am your Medea, and I
    Will never disappoint Our
    Expectations of Fame and its
    Omnipotent Fist. [*Pause.*] How the day goes.
    I will execute the vengeance
    Due, and its fall-out will rain
    Acidly on any woman who
    Dares take out our way of life.

    [M.J. *exits into the house.*]

CHORUS: Fly, fly, sails and planes. Flow back
    To the source; restore the status.
    Women are deceitful, their vows
    Are loose. Men must be paid their dues.
Stop the love-songs, stop the singing,
    Or I'll answer the opposite sex:
    It's not a happy ending; it's
    Either boredom or betrayal.
From the bombed-out inner-city,
    He radiated for all men;
    His strengths jumped exponentially
    With every task and contest won.

CHORUS: [*Cont'd.*] He left a mother and a first

    Wife, with his glittering torso,

    For her. The woman doesn't know

    The meaning of sacrifices.

    In America, a sense of

    Shame should blot out the sun, and make

    Every unfaithful bed cold, cold,

    Cold. Vows are vows, and lies are lies.

    [*Pause; the* CHORUS *indulges in self-congratulatory asides.*]

MRS. MEDEA: [*Entering on motorcycle, accompanied by an entourage of attractive motorcycle-riding L.A.-types. The revving of this group's engines may punctuate the ensuing dialogue between* M.J. *and the* MRS., *or, the* MRS. *might flash a signal which results in their silence.*]

    This isn't the first time I've heard men yabba

    Yabba yabba-ing about things they make up in

    Their heads. Shut up. Get a life. You know nothing here

    About nothing here. There's two sides to a story.

    And what does your pledge mean? 'Til death do us part? Ha.

    More like another woman's panties on the floor.

    Sacrifice? Don't make me laugh. [*She laughs.*] Are you kid
        ding?

    I know a thing or two about "great" men, and the fibs behind

    Them. Men lie and it's called second nature.

    Cute. To be expected. Women lie and they're dirt.

    My children will NOT be raised to believe this, or

    To perpetuate the sickness in your heads. Go!

    Get Medea for me. I want him to hear this.

CHORUS: [*Pause; shifting uncomfortably, then loftily.*] It's a strange
    form of anger, difficult to cure,
    When those with fortune turn hatred upon themselves.

MRS.: Oh I know how men like you think. Understand?

  Don't bother changing your tune for me.

  Ok? I'm not buyin' it. Save it for your wives.

  And don't you dare talk down to me. Go fuck yourselves.

  [M.J. *enters from the house without being called.*]

M.J.: I thought I heard the unmistakable tone of

  White trash. Whatever you want, take it elsewhere, tramp.

MRS.: [*A bit cowed initially by his presence, but bouncing back fast.*]
  You know what I'm here for, your two spoiled brats; but

  First things first. My sources tell me you want to give

  Me a hard time over my right to divorce. Now

  Listen; it makes no sense. You don't want me. Right?

  We should both let each other go. And for the sake of

  The kids, we should act like adults, and try to get

  Along. Ok? I'm sick, sore and tired of this,

  And that's putting it mildly. Ok? What are

  We fighting for, anyway? It's ridiculous.

  Let's stop the insanity, and do the right thing,

  I'll take my half and leave you in peace. Whatever.

M.J.: Be careful woman; I'll tell you the way it is.

  You're mine and you always will be. It doesn't matter

  If I don't want you or if I do. You have no rights.

  Period. End of story. I'll take care of that.

  And your beef with my behavior? It's not

  Your place to complain. It's enough to have touched me.

  Every American adores ME not you, uh?

  And they have their inalienable right to revere

  ME, without your petty interferences. Babe,

  You coulda learned a few new tricks from their acts.

MRS.: I don't quite see things like that. To hear it from you,

I've never given you my worship; how untrue.

You know, the charisma of a zeus can turn a girl's head.

I wanted you. You were like, a king, surrounded

By awe; you got the best seats, the best smiles, the

Best sensational press. I wanted to be part

Of you too. But I found out that wasn't your game.

Yeah, you married me, but never made me a queen.

No. You were the gold, and I was the brass. Well now, as

You see, I've got my own devotees, and they do

Whatever I ask. Not your kind of crowd, yet no

One's really what they appear to be, right, M.J.?

M.J.: There oughta be a brand on women to tell the

True from the false. You're at least a two-headed one.

You'll never be anything more than the trashy

Waitress you were when I met you. You shoulda been

Grateful for every night you got your claws around

Me. Your tickets for steak started here, along with

Meals at my table for all your hangers-on.

You're a disease. You think you can take me down, with

Your tabloid tits and your low-life cohorts. Think again.

MRS.: I coulda had my pick of men; you weren't exactly

Hurt by the young beautiful blonde on your arm.

M.J.: It's bleached.

MRS.: So what?

M.J.: You're a witch.

MRS.: Can I talk?

M.J.: Know your place, woman. You weren't meant to talk back.

MRS.: I have a mind, if you hadn't noticed, it's mine.

M.J.: NO. I gave you all the life you were entitled to.

If you were meant to get any more bliss from life's

Bank, it woulda come from me, when I gave the word.

MRS.: Jealousy from you is hypocritical,

Dontcha think?

Change your ideas, cantcha?

Obedience and your

Possessiveness are out of style.

Get with it. Realize: women

Aren't dogs; neither are wives

Cows with rings through their fingers.

M.J.: I come into a room, you

Should be turning to see me.

I step out, you should be waiting.

I'd like to hear the sound

Of my voice: Play it back for me.

MRS.: Better. Here's a mirror for you.

Knock yourself out. Go for it.

M.J.: To love, honor and obey.

MRS.: You mocked those words first, not me.

M.J.: The only proof is your lies.

MRS.: My lies? The one you cherish

Is you, and always will be. [*Pause.*]

They're all watching for your fall,

Ya know. The only thing they'll

Feel is relief not to have been

Stars themselves, and bound to explode.

[*Pause; they turn their backs on one another.*]

CHORUS: Although the things she says sound sort

    Of reasonable . . . Still I think,

    Though you might not agree, she has

    Wronged Medea and acted badly.

    Anyway, we don't care about the

    Woman or what she says. We want

    To find out what happens to our

    Hero. It's his story that makes

    Us shudder, that makes us moan, or

    Groan. Maybe we do want to project

    Ourselves into his fate and

    Live vicariously. So what?

M.J.: DON'T YOU EVER TURN YOUR BACK ON ME DO
YOU HEAR. [*Pause.*]

MRS.: Look. Let's make a deal. Of course I still want you.

    That is, more like, I want to be in your party;

    I want my own bliss; I want to be on a throne;

    I want the same special treatment. Please. Let me

    Finish. Sure, I went after you; what girl wouldn't?

    You were a god to like, the whole world. But now I know

    You're all too human. Ok? You're a man like

    Any other, and you can't control me; you don't own

    Me. Wait. This is it. Make me a goddess, equal

    To your level, and I promise I'll worship you

    Like everyone else; erotically, neurotically,

    Whatever you want. Only, no more screwing

    Around; no more reminding me of my dependent

    Place. Can't you see, we need each other, M.J.

MRS.: [*Cont'd.*] And I wanna be just as important as you.

M.J.: You're a fool. You're crazy. No one cares about you.
You're off the deep end if you think you can try to
Manipulate ME. I've got the power to prove
You'll be sorry, bitch. I'll see this world dead before
I cave to your, to any woman's demands. You're nuts.
You're here to take orders, not give them. Get it.

MRS.: What's the point. This is useless.

M.J.: You got that right, and how. I
Read you like a see-through book.

MRS.: You're stubborn and arrogant.

M.J.: AND THAT'S WHY YOU FELL FOR ME.

MRS.: I was young then, and stupid.

M.J.: ENOUGH. Go on. GET OUT. I've been
More than patient, listening to you.
Another thing you're too selfish
To see. Your time's up. Get lost. NOW.
What are you waiting for, uh? GO!

MRS.: Fine. I don't need this abuse.
But send out the children. They're
Coming with me. I won't see them growing up to —

M.J.: NO. You WILL SEE. You will see what the future holds.
Soon enough, woman. You're temporary. And MY
Children? They're staying with ME. I know you. You'll get
Sick of 'em and ship 'em back in NO TIME at all.

MRS.: That's not true! They're half mine too! Everything is, well,
Just like the money should be. Why can't you share with—

M.J.: [*Laughing loudly.*]

> HALF? HA. What's mine will RUIN you. What's mine will
> STARVE YOU. Poison bitch. What's mine. Is mine. THAT
> matters.

MRS.: I don't know why you have to get so angry. I did

> Some important things for you. I got you into
> Places. The best places. Circles for only the
> Beautiful and you know what I mean. When we first
> Met you were just another jock. But with me you —

M.J.: With YOU. With WHO? Where do you get the gas to
pump

> This shit? Somethin's gettin' you higher than your height.

MRS.: You never appreciated me. You never

> Valued what I gave to you. Not even the kids —

M.J.: THE CHILDREN ARE MINE. All children belong to
men.

MRS.: What are you saying? I have no rights, period?

M.J.: She walks. She talks. Maybe she has a brain in there.

> How many blondes does it take to change a light bulb?

MRS.: That does it. You and your friends think your egos

> Are above even the laws of this land? Well, I'll
> Prove that's a hoax too, just like you. Inferior?
> Subordinate? Stupid? You just wait. Hahaha.

M.J.: I WOULDN'T LAUGH IF I WERE YOU. IF YOU
WERE A

> FORTUNE-TELLER YOU'D BE SCARED ABOUT
> NOW GODDAMN
> YOU. NO. YOU WAIT. YOU ARE WAITING. YEAH.
> FOR NOTHIN'.

MRS.: No one. Not TV, not the trades, not the children

Will think you The Man when I'm through exposing you.

You're not the god you think you are. Whoring around

For advertisers. Selling some faded image

To prop-up your castle. This system's about to

Go down. Get ready for the crash M.J. But first,

Send out the kids. I'm their mother. And I want them.

With me. They won't be reared with your idiocy.

M.J.: YOU DON'T GET IT DO YOU. MY CHILDREN? I'D SEE THEM

DEAD BEFORE I'D LET YOU HAVE 'EM. THAT'S RIGHT. I'D KILL

THEM MYSELF TO STOP YOU. HALF? HALF. YOU WANT HALF? HA.

YOU'RE NOTHING. NOTHING. I'M WHAT MAT TERS. ME. ME. MY

GOLDEN VOICE. Shall I sing you THE BALLAD OF HOLLIS

BROWN, baby? Or the one about the dude in

Long Island who blew his whole family away?

Nah. I don't wanna spoil the show. I hate it

When somebody gives away the plot. NOW GET LOST.

BE GONE. THERE'S PRECIOUS FEW BREATHS TO WASTE TIL THE END .

MRS.: What are you saying? It doesn't have to be this

Way. God why couldn't I have had a normal life.

M.J.: [*Laughs.*] OH IT'S WAY TOO LATE FOR THAT. GO WHILE YOU STILL CAN.

BUT YOU BETTER GO REAL FAR. WAY FAR FROM HERE. AND

M.J.: [*Cont'd.*] IF YOU DON'T, IF YOU THINK YOU CAN
BRING MY LIFE TO

YOUR FEET, THEN YOU BEST KISS THE THINGS —
AND WE ALL KNOW

THEY'RE THINGS YOU LOVE GOODBYE. SAY BYE-
BYE BLOOD SUCKER.

MRS.: I don't know what you're talking about. We could've

Been so good together. If only you would see—

M.J.: OH I SEE. I SEE THE PAST. I SEE THE FUTURE.

AND I AM THOSE. I KNOW WHAT YOU WANTED
ME FOR.

MRS.: You're becoming a real loser M.J. I never

Thought I'd hear you feeling sorry for yourself.

I'm above that. And people'll worship me

For myself. I don't need you. Or your money.

And eventually the law'll side with me too.

M.J.: WE'LL SEE WHO'S WEAK. YOU WANNA FIGHT.
YOU GOT IT GIRL.

THESE HANDS KNOW. KNOW WHO AND HOW IT'S
GONNA FALL OUT.

MRS.: We'll see.

M.J.: OH YEAH.

MRS.: Fine.

M.J.: Right. GET OUT. I'M SICK OF YOU.

> [*Exit* MRS. MEDEA *with her entourage.* M.J. *paces. Long pause.
> The* CHORUS *shifts uncomfortably, then regroups.*]

CHORUS: In matters of love, and in

Matters of money, learn this:

Desire in excess is AIDS like

Nothing else. If love can heal,

CHORUS: [*Cont'd.*] The opposite is true. Hatred

Can shatter and greed can kill.

The best marriage is a boring

And dispassionate one; it makes

For a peaceful home. Ah! let my

Emotions be harnessed just so!

But realistically, we

Are men, and what we want at

Home, we seldom want in bed!

[*General laughter amongst the chorus.*]

It's true. But with every seduction,

A later rejection is implied.

And as far as this story goes,

The public is always hungry

To eat a tasty Donald Trump. Yeah.

And why not? If a god has clay

Feet, then a man needs friends.

To be a celebrity

Is a nice fantasy, but

To be a regular guy means

Never to sink from fame. If

A man never knows the crests and peaks

Of grace, he'll be saved a

Drowning in anonymity.

M.J.: [*Pacing and muttering.*]

Women. MEN! Do you see how she believes she can

Exploit me. ME!? I AM NOT IN DECLINE. WHAT.
WHAT?!

NO-O-O-O-O-O-O-O-O-O-O-O-O.

M.J.: [*Cont'd.*] MEN. You heard her threats and half-baked plans.
  Now I say,

Whatever happens she brings on herself. SHE LOVES IT.

Medea. MEDEA. The worship of CONTROL.

A man's children are HIS; his blood, his line, his

PRESERVE. In my image. In my mind. What I am.

SHOWS. NO. WEAKNESS. For in his domain is he de
  fined:

OURS. THE MAN who stopped not raising himself up.

FOR OUR WORLD MEN. The Man will now DEFEND
  us.

It's a sacrifice I take on with THE FORCE OF

THE U.S. MARINES. THE EMPEROR STRIKES BACK.
  Yes.

He will call on the four winds. He will summon the

Powers dark and the powers light, and the henchmen,

The real men, of our man's world, will not hesitate

To play their rightfully righteous positions

For our man's game. For you, men. THE MAN. Who is HE?

MEE-EE-EE-EE EEE EE-EE-EE-EE-EE-EEEEEEEEEE.

  [*The* CHORUS *shifts awkwardly; long pause.* M.J. *dances. Enter
  the* BEST FRIEND.]

BEST FRIEND: Hey, I saw your ugly mug all over the covers

Of the scandal-sheets, man. What's up with that shit?

M.J.: My brother. Where ya been, sport? I need my back-up.

FRIEND: I guess so, man. The press is gonna eat you

Alive. And so is the public, man. Kiss the

Endorsements goodbye. Not to mention that high cloud

You sit on. If you drop, how far down, man. How far.

M.J.: I'm gonna put a stop to her way before that.

FRIEND: How far can she rock you, man? It's probably nothin'.

M.J.: I'll see to that. Don't fret. This'll be some good shit now.

FRIEND: The women these days. Always tryin'to make the

World shift out from under our feet. I like them when

They're young and stupid, man. Know what I mean. Pussy.

[*Pause.*] Life's no cakewalk for me, neither. But I'm listening.

M.J.: You've got troubles, it's true. But I've gotcha covered.

FRIEND: I've got alimony, too. I've gotta think

Of myself. I need a pay-off, with no jail time.

M.J.: Not to worry, Jack. *Mi casa es su casa.*

FRIEND: So what's your plan, man? I know the bitch's schedule.

M.J.: HOW'S THAT?

FRIEND: The dame's been makin' the rounds, M.J. That's it.

M.J.: [*After a pause.*] Don't' sweat it. I'll tell you everything impor
tant when

You need to know. A man is judged by his actions.

If you help, I'll protect you. If not, you're free; go.

FRIEND: How can you question my loyalty. I'M HERE.

M.J.: You swear to do anything I ask, regardless?

FRIEND: Relax, M.J. I'm your back-up. [*Pause.*] I swear, alright?

M.J.: What happens to guys who back down on their pledges?

FRIEND: We all know they're nothin' but women, God help 'em.

M.J.: Enough. I won't forget it. Or you. Now wait for

Me in the trophy room, and prepare yourself well.

[*The BEST FRIEND exits into the house; M.J. paces slowly.*]

CHORUS: Each fissure in the old world

Requires a new boot. Sure,

Nostalgia is natural; too is

Defending our way of life.

CHORUS: [*Cont'd.*] M.J. protects us; he acts

   Through us, for us on our behalf.

   If he's tarnished so aren't we.

   No. Whatever he chooses,

   We must uphold him. Failure

   Is not an option. How can we change?

M.J.: MEN. Revenge will hit the freeways; San Pedro is

   My harbor; I'm about to launch my plot. Now for

   The whole idea; wait, don't speak. I've thought this through

   Completely. NOW ALL OUT with its wrath. To swing it

   Straight from this height, like the guillotine, the pitchfork

   The scythe. Medea, Medea, Medea MINE.

   She'll nourish. Feeding my eyes with her velvet blood.

   A gushing murder of the constellations.

   After all, we can't get away from violence in

   America. [*He laughs.*] I'll play the grieving Hollywood

   Legend. It is sad, for things to come to this.

   BUT I WILL NOT BE BROUGHT DOWN TO HER.
      And ALL children

   WILL grow to adore me. Our ways ascendant, uh?

   Not bad. And the sympathy won't hurt my stock. Nope.

   I'm forever loved; this is just a small growth spurt.

   Painful, perhaps, but I've already decided.

   That's that. I know you're with me. So tallyho, boys.

   It's not enough to stew and brood on our fury;

   It's time for the future that I make. I TAKE.

   She must die! Or else she betrays me, and all men!

      [M.J. *prepares to exit;* CHORUS *pipes up quickly.*]

CHORUS: But the mother of your children? Think
　　Of the kiddies' deprivation, shouldn't you?

M.J.: They'll forget. They'll have me.

CHORUS: Hmm ... Perhaps civilization has
　　Some advantages. You could control
　　Yourself. It might be better.

M.J.: That's easy for you to say.
　　You live on the ground. I'm cut way
　　Above. YOU EXPECT ME TO GANGWAY?

CHORUS: Of course not. Still, now that you've shared
　　Your plans with us, why not reconsider?

M.J.: She's a vessel, that's all; she doesn't matter.
　　Who cares about her. One more aging female, the
　　Scourge of our Earth. I'm doing a public service.

CHORUS: It's murder. Can it be forgotten
　　At the drop of night? More likely,
　　You'll relive it when you look at
　　Their little faces. You'll see yourself
　　A murderer. And come on, you'll
　　Remember their mother's blood.

M.J.: NO. It's my blood that counts, you wimps. Aren't you men?
　　NO. You're whipped. And that's the difference between us,
　　uh?

　　　[M.J. *exits into the house.*]

CHORUS: [*After clearing their throats.*]
　　Once upon a time, yeah, men came
　　From across the globe to harness
　　The bounties of this continent;
　　They carved cities, roads, towns and farms

CHORUS: [*Cont'd.*] Like nothin' ever seen before.
    History flew ten times fast, faster
    Still; men drew up sweet-sounding
    Documents for liberty, justice;
    Laws created to improve
    Society. The lady with
    The scales is beautiful, man,
    Because she's a picture of civilized
    Equality. In reality,
    Things didn't always factor out
    So fair, but the ideal
    Lives on, and needs our protection.
    M.J.,if you willfully kill,
    How will you live within this country?
    Murder is against all principles
    Of freedom and independence.
    It's wrong; it'll change you, it'll
    Change your life. But you'll have to
    See for yourself it seems. Like all
    Men, we only realize afterwards
    What's right. The desire for
    Dominance is a strong one, no doubt.
    But we must be more than this, right?
    Stop yourself. Don't do it, M.J.
        [M.J. *enters from the house.*]
M.J.: Who's ruling here, girls? You sound like so many tamed
    Animals. WhatRya? Gettin' laid and gettin' used to it;
    Lettin' yourselves be led around by the heads. Which ones?

M.J.: [*Cont'd.*] I'm not surprised. But with the way they want to make

You into robots and machines, can't you see, they

Deserve what they get; they're askin' for it, in fact.

When they yak their twisted ballyhoo at us, well,

They're damned lucky not to get slapped or screamed at.

Yeah, they're wrapped up in their way, but you don't hafta

Agree. Get a spine. No woman's gonna fuck me or make

Me think like her. If you spoil them like that, they'll

Just wanna go higher. My ex is evidence

Of female ambition. What a hoot. A dime a dozen.

The ordinariness of bimbos after

A few years can't be hidden by dark glasses

Or all sorts of lotion; one face is as good or

As bad as another. Should you do what they say

So THEY'LL be satisfied with YOU? I DON'T THINK SO.

That's not what I'm here for, or you. NOW WATCH as I

Show you the stuff of the myths. There's more I could say,

But I'm tired of this. Just look what they're doing.

To you, but NEVER ME. I've got the iron hand. Look-n-learn

From THE MASTER. This ain't no bullshit magazine.

[*M.J. snaps his fingers. The* BEST FRIEND *enters from the house. The two men exit the stage together,* M.J. *leads.*]

CHORUS: [*After a pause.*]

A man wants a diamond, and thinks about nothing

Else. The color, cut, size, weight and cost of the stone

Takes up all of his considerations. He strives

And saves and plots and cheats and competes for the rock.

CHORUS: [*Cont'd.*] He knows, he believes, when he finally holds
    the
    Gem in his hand, he will be happy, and want for
    Nought. One day, the diamond is his. He mounts it, on
    A ring, on an arm-charm. It sparkles, it glitters;
    He glows from inside. He shines it, he cleans it, he
    Tucks it into its velvet box. He's happy.
    Then one day the worries begin. What if it's lost.
    What if he's mugged for it. What if, while crossing a
    Street, his rock slides away, and into the gutter,
    Falling through the sewers and into the sea. What
    If, even when locked within its red-velvet pouch,
    He returns home to find it violated. What
    Will he do without it? What will he do without
    The trappings of himself, without the things of his
    Self that he believes make up him?

> [*Pause. Night falls. The sound of one lonely dog barking. Pause. A limousine slowly enters. It appears to be driving itself. It stops in front of the house. Pause. Lights fade up slowly to the loud sounds of birds and/or an urban cacophony, which ceases abruptly when three lawyers dart from the automobile. The* LAWYERS *are dressed in expensive suits. A group of* MEDIA *rush on stage and surround the vehicle/lawyers.* THE MEDIA *shouts ad-libbed questions until the lawyers respond.*]

MEDIA: Where's M.J.? Where's M.J.? Where is he?
    Do you know where he is? Can you tell us anything?

THE THREE LAWYERS: Mr. Medea has no comment, no comment,
    No comment, please. Ladies and gentlemen, please.

MEDIA: We aren't leaving. The public has
    A right to know. M.J.! Where is
    He? What does he have to say now?

MEDIA: [*Cont'd.*] Will he come out and speak to us?

M.J., M.J.? Where is he? Where?

LAWYERS: Please, please. Mr. Medea plans to cooperate

Fully with the authorities. He will be —

  [M.J. *appears, climbing the house-walls/scaffolding. He is drenched in blood. Everyone is momentarily stunned. The* LAWYERS *go into a huddle and many cameras flash.*]

MEDIA: M.J.! M.J.! How does it feel?

Tell us M.J.! We still love you!

We want your point of view! M.J.!

Over here! M.J.! Talk to us!

LAWYERS: Mr. Medea will not be making a statement

At this time. Please. Allow us to consult with —

  [M.J. *continues to climb; blood drips.*]

M.J.: I AM MEDEA. I AM MEDEA. The woman

Is mine, MINE. So now she knows; now you all know.

Who the fuck cares. No one laughs at me. I showed her,

You, all men, me, I AM DEBASED. NO! Can't slip. Can't.

THE ROCK, I will NOT fail. Am not falling WILL NOT.

MEDIA: This'll sell the commercial spots.

Wow. Get it all. M.J.! M.J.!

Over here M.J.! M.J.! M.J.!

The cops say her throat was slit

Like a pig's. Any comment on this?

M.J.! M.J.! Talk to us! Tell —

M.J.: Who says she's dead? SHE'S NOT dead until I SAY!

Take a good look at me. [*Pause.*] SHE DIED OF YOUR
    OWN DISEASE!

Thou art on thy deathbed. Down Strumpet! It's too late!

MEDIA: Can you answer some questions for

Us, M.J.? M.J.? Medea!

If you give us an exclusive,

Well, we'll see, we'll talk. Who knows how

High the brass'll pay for this dish.

Whaddaya say M.J.? M.J.?

LAWYERS: As your lawyers, we advise:

Say no more, or they'll kill you M.J.

M.J.: A MAN'S SKIN CAN BE BURNED AWAY BY THE
    FIRES

OF HELL BUT THE COURAGE TO AVENGE HIM
    SELF MAKES

A MAN IMMORTAL LIKE THE GODS. I AM FLYING.

MEDIA: Did you get that? Did you catch it?

No matter what, we'll get our story.

And what a story, holy cow.

Play the race card; play the battery.

It's pure Americana.

M.J.: OH SHE WAS SURPRISED. Never thought. I'd spring.
    Knew she

Had NOT the weapon to make me a beggar. NO!

The long white neck. The most beautiful eyes. Murder.

Her eyes, widening, Then OUT out out out. My wife.

I HAVE NO WIFE. NEED NONE. Nothing. BRING ME
    THE CHECK!

Only I have money to burn! Only I have.

LAWYERS: It'll be two mistrials and a

Plea bargain. Time served. No jury

Will slap the fate of conviction

On any rich celebrity.

M.J.: [*Climbing higher, hounded by the press.*]

Women don't have souls. That was proven by

St. Augustine a helluva long time ago. She knew.

She knew that too. Everyone loved me. After all.

Maybe I didn't kill her. And if I say I

Didn't, then I didn't. I'll believe it myself.

I decide, I decide what to DO SAY THINK BE.

AND NO ONE CAN TOUCH ME. No one can touch me
now.

MEDIA: Are you getting this? Get it ALL.

M.J., over here. M.J.! M.J.!

Hey, Medea! What's the matter?

Didn't she give good head?

[*General loud laughter amongst the members of* THE MEDIA.]

M.J.: Oh, She was foul! Whose breath these hands have newly
stopped!

Horrible. But no. I'll become richer now. MORE!

[*Hysterical laughter.*]

These Americans. This sky. My fans. HE IS WHAT.

LAWYERS: We're outta here. See ya in court.

We'll do lunch. Or catch us on

Entertainment Tonight. It's his, his-

Story, but it's our dough. Right.

We'll soak him. We'll get our fees.

First'll be the book, and then all

Our royalties. What's next? The best

Parties in high society!

[LAWYERS *move to exit;* M.J. *climbs; the scaffolding bursts into
flames. The* LAWYERS *do not exit; they, and all the cast, watch. The
flames rise.*]

M.J.: No. I had to. Or fall. Killing her, I fell. No. This

Falling isn't. Is it. I am not. He is what.

It's still all me. All about me. All. I am not.

All. My verge of. Nothing. I am not. He is what.

DON'T SHOOT UNTIL YOU SEE THE WHITES OF THEIR whatnot.

I can't look back. Won't. Plunge. No. KILL THE MESSEN-GER.

[M.J. *burns.* THE MEDIA *films/photographs. All cast-members who previously exited now enter.* M.J. *burns, climbs higher, then out of sight.*]
[*Enter the* STREET PREACHER.]

STREET PREACHER: Repent I say! No man is guilty! Jesus saves!

[*As the fire burns out,* THE MEDIA *can be seen interviewing* THE HOUSE BOY, THE CHAUFFEUR, THE LAWYERS *and* THE BEST FRIEND. THE POLICEMEN *pick haphazardly through the wreckage.* THE PREACHER *hands out pamphlets, etc. The following dialogue may be played separately or layered simultaneously.*]

MEDIA: Get the Chauffeur! Get 'im before

He leaves! Lighting! Sound! Over here!

Mr. Chauffeur! Mr. Chauffeur!

Tell us your side of the story!

CHAUFFEUR: I saw nothin'. Get your cotton

Pickin' hands offa me. What the...

Wait. Whatsit to ya? Huh? How much?

How much am I gonna git for it?

MEDIA: House Boy, House Boy. Come on kid, give.

HOUSE BOY: Well, Mr. Medea was

Never easy to work for, that's for

Sure. But that's because he was like

One of those Aztecs, man. Fire

HOUSE BOY: [*Cont'd.*] And Ice. Oh yeah, I was close to
The Man, sure. I loved working for
A Star. Ya never know, working
For them, what's gonna happen to
You. It could be like the Lotto.
Sure, I dream a little dream. Why
The hell not? Why else work for such
Snots. No. We were very close. I
Loved the Boss. He always told me
All of his secrets. What? I can't
Tell you that! They're priceless, the
Stories I have on our Medea.

MEDIA: 50 grand! 80! A mil!
What can I authorize for this?
Get me a hookup with Murdoch! Now!

[THE LAWYERS *and* THE BEST FRIEND *attempt to exit; they are swamped by cameras, etc.*]

LAWYERS: No comment. No comment now. No.
Read the book. It'll be out soon.

[THE LAWYERS *exit.* THE BEST FRIEND *pushes past all without talking.* THE STREET PREACHER *attempts to leaflet them before they exit.* THE MEDIA *changes its focus to* THE POLICEMEN, *who have been picking clumsily through the chaos.* THE MEDIA *ad-libs questions to* THE POLICE. THE POLICEMAN *who did most of the speaking earlier steps forward. He holds up his hands dramatically to quiet the press.*]

POLICEMAN: [*Deliberately.*] I'm speakin' . . . under the
Condition . . . of a-non-y-mi-ty.

[*General, loud laughter from all present.*]
[*Continue ad-lib dialogues between* THE MEDIA *and their*

interview subjects. Also ad-lib intra-police and intra-media confer-
encing. A widespread hubbub as the CHORUS *begins its final passage.*]

CHORUS: Is heaven the overseer of all our doings?

What we think, and what we expect, are not confirmed.

Once upon a time, a big black bear was poor and

Despised, yet he grew up to be our hero.

We, who needed an idol, both feared and cherished

Him; and we built him to the skies. In fact, his

Violence dwelled also within us, and, in terms of

His authority to tyrannize us, well, we sorta

Lived through him. It's true. But if no animal is

An island, then similarly, no creature is

Beyond reproach. Thus we, who placed Medea in

Repose, are as much to blame for this mess. Uh-huh.

It's difficult to say just why we've done this. Yeah.

Money changes everything. But when anybody's

Excesses are tolerated to the point of

Destruction, then we create our own Monsters;

Our Medeas. And so it is in this story.

Rich Orloff

I DIDN'T KNOW
YOU COULD COOK

I Didn't Know You Could Cook by Rich Orloff. Copyright © 1997 by Rich Orloff. All rights reserved. Reprinted by permission of Bret Adams, Ltd.

CAUTION: Professionals and amateurs are hereby warned that *I Didn't Know You Could Cook* by Rich Orloff is subject to a royalty. It is fully protected under the copyright laws of the United States of America, and of all countries covered by the International Copyright Union (including the Dominion of Canada and the rest of the British Commonwealth), and of all countries covered by the Pan-American Convention and the Universal Copyright Convention, and of all countries with which the United States has reciprocal copyright relations. All rights, including professional, amateur, motion picture, recitation, lecturing, public reading, radio broadcasting, television, video or sound taping, all other forms of mechanical or electronic reproduction, such as information storage and retrieval systems and photocopying, and the rights of translation into foreign languages, are strictly reserved. Particular emphasis is placed upon the question of readings, permission for which must be secured from the author's agent in writing.

All inquiries should be addressed to Bret Adams, Ltd.; 448 West 44th Street; New York, NY 10036; Attention: Melissa Hardy.

Rich Orloff

Rich Orloff's plays have been seen at such regional theaters as American Stage Company in New Jersey, Arizona Theatre Company, Florida Studio Theatre, the Bathhouse Theatre in Seattle, Philadelphia Festival Theatre for New Plays, and the Key West Theatre Festival. His full-length plays include the comedies *Veronica's Position* (winner, 1995 New Plays in America Festival), *Damaged Goods* (winner, 1995 Festival of Firsts), *Someone's Knocking*, *Water Boy*, and the drama *Days of Possibilities*, based on true stories of college life during the Vietnam era.

His many one-acts include *The Whole Shebang*, which was published in *The Best American Short Plays 1994-5*, and which has since received over thirty productions in theaters and schools throughout the country. His short play *August Afternoon* was recently published as part of *Ten-Minute Plays from Actors Theatre of Louisville, Volume Four*.

I Didn't Know You Could Cook began as a ten-minute play for the National Theatre Workshop of the Handicapped. Expanded and revised, the play was produced by the Carousel Theatre Company in New York along with two more of Rich's one-act comedies, *Oedi* and *Mars Needs Women But Not as Much as Arnold Schecter*, under the umbrella title *Sexy People*. That production of *Cook* was directed by Vicki Meisner and featured William-Kevin Young and Christopher Kirk Allen. The play was also produced in the spring of 1977 by the Sackett Group, directed by Valerie Harris, and featured Kelly AuCoin and Dan Haft.

The author would like to give special thanks to Rick Curry, artistic director of the National Theatre Workshop of the Handicapped, and to the actors in that company, whose experiences and talent inspired this play.

CHARACTERS

JEROME   mid-20's, paraplegic, uses a wheelchair

MARK   near 30, his older brother

SETTING: *The kitchen of a modest urban apartment.*

TIME: *Dinner time.*

NOTE: *In a kitchen used by someone confined to a wheelchair, the higher shelves would be empty, and all appliances would be in easy reach.*

As the play begins, JEROME *and* MARK *are at the kitchen table finishing dinner.* JEROME *has gone to some effort to make the meal setting look classy.*

MARK: Anyway, so he pulls up to the stoplight, and he begins revving up his little Corvette engine, and I think, give me a break.

JEROME: Uh-huh.

MARK: I didn't get my Porsche to be macho or anything. I just like how it feels.

JEROME: Uh-huh.

MARK: But he keeps revving his engine, rhhm, rhhm, rhhmmmm, so, so right before the light changes, I roll down my window —

JEROME: Yeah.

MARK: And I say, "I think you've done a wonderful job of compensating for a small penis."

JEROME: You didn't.

MARK: Light changed; I took off; left him in the dust.

JEROME: Wow, it's so cool they gave you a Porsche as a bonus.

MARK: Hey, if you ever want to get into sales . . .

JEROME: I think I'll stick with teaching.

MARK: Well, if you ever want me to help. After all, what's a brother for?

JEROME: Thanks. Not that I could drive one, anyway.

MARK: I'm sure they could adjust it.

JEROME: Bucket seats? Low to the ground? I think I'll stick with my Ford.

MARK: I'm sure they could adjust anything, if you pay them enough.

JEROME: I'll stick with my Ford. We've developed a very intimate and trusting relationship.

MARK: You know, in a just world, they'd give teachers cars as bonuses.

JEROME: That'll be the day.

MARK: Well, you work hard enough for it.

JEROME: I'm just glad they finally put all the ramps up.

MARK: I thought they had to do that years ago.

JEROME: They did.

MARK: Then why didn't they?

JEROME: They hadn't run out of excuses yet.

MARK: [*Finishing eating.*] This was delicious, Jerome. Absolutely delicious.

JEROME: I'm glad you liked it.

MARK: I'm really impressed. I didn't know you could cook.

JEROME: Millions of people can cook, Mark. Maybe billions.

MARK: Not me. I tried making pasta once; a couple of pieces are still stuck to my wall.

JEROME: Would you like some dessert?

MARK: Oh, no, I'm stuffed.

JEROME: It's chocolate mousse pie. Made it from scratch.

MARK: Sorry. No room.

JEROME: You don't need room for chocolate mousse pie. It just fills the crevices around the food you've already eaten.

MARK: Can't do it. I've already met my caloric maximum for the day.

JEROME: I forgot how disciplined you are.

MARK: Even a small paunch can negatively impact a woman's first response to you.

JEROME: I'll remember that.

MARK: Besides, I, I probably should be heading back to the hotel.

JEROME: It's early.

MARK: I know, but I have another meeting first thing in the —

JEROME: [*Overlapping with the above.*] But we've hardly —

MARK: [*Overlapping with the above.*] They didn't fly me this far so I could —

JEROME: [*Overlapping with the above.*] I just hoped we could —

MARK: [*Overlapping with the above.*] Next time I'm in town —

JEROME: Right. Sure.

MARK: Hey.

JEROME: You know — you know how long it's been since we've spent any real time together?

MARK: Six months?

JEROME: Five years.

MARK: What do you mean? I saw you at Mom's birthday thing, and Uncle Ted and Aunt Lisa's fiftieth anniversary, and at Daniel's wedding.

JEROME: Those are family things. Nobody really talks at them.

MARK: Sure, they do.

JEROME: Mark, the reason they're called family *functions* is because that's about all you can do at them.

MARK: Well, we've talked the last hour, haven't we?

JEROME: Yeah. I guess. [JEROME *starts taking the dishes to the kitchen sink.*]

MARK: Can I help with the —

JEROME: I got it.

MARK: I'd be glad to —

JEROME: I got it . . . Would you like some coffee?

MARK: Caffeine after seven? Never.

JEROME: I have decaf.

MARK: I really can't stay —

JEROME: Right.

MARK: Hey, Mom sent me that article about you in the paper.

JEROME: About the disabled schoolteacher all the third graders adore?

MARK: It was a good article.

JEROME: It was your generic "Let's admire the handicapped" piece. They just filled in the blanks with my name.

MARK: Nobody writes about me.

JEROME: Look, it was a fine article; I, I just don't like being

JEROME: [*Cont'd.*] written up because I can do what people *assume* I can't do. If they were honest, the piece would have been titled, "Local Crip Transcends Expectations."

MARK: Well, *I* liked the piece.

JEROME: I'm glad.

MARK: And even if this isn't... correct, I'm really impressed by how well you've learned to manage on your own.

JEROME: And I'm impressed by how well you've learned to manage on your own, too, Mark.

MARK: All I mean is, well, I never thought you'd move out and live on your own. I mean, I knew you could. I knew you could do anything you put your mind to.

JEROME: I think professional ski jumping is out.

MARK: Well, anything practical.

JEROME: The jumping I could finesse; it's the lifts that frighten me.

MARK: I'm still proud of what you've done. I'm sorry if that bugs you, but it's true.

JEROME: I haven't done anything special.

MARK: I'm not sure I could have done what you've done.

JEROME: You just haven't been tested.

MARK: Still, to live alone when you're, well, you know — I think it's quite an accomplishment.

JEROME: Well, it's not like I'm completely alone.

MARK: Why? Is someone hiding in the bedroom or something?

JEROME: No, no, it's just, well, to quote Ringo, or was it George, anyway, to quote one of them, I get by with a little help from my friends.

MARK: Oh, does some social agency help —

JEROME: No, I mean friends. You know, *friends.*

MARK: I know, *friends.* The people you put in your Rolodex who aren't business connections.

JEROME: I also, um, well, I, there's, there's also one special friend.

MARK: No, really?

JEROME: Really.

MARK: Who?

JEROME: Oh, just... just someone special.

MARK: Who?

JEROME: Well —

MARK: What's her name?

JEROME: Louie.

MARK: Louie?

JEROME: Louie.

MARK: Well, if there can be an actress named Glenn Close, I guess there can be a woman named Louie.

JEROME: Louie's a man.

MARK: Oh, so he's just a friend.

JEROME: We're more than friends.

MARK: He's a good friend.

JEROME: We're more than good friends.

MARK: He's a good, good friend.

JEROME: We're lovers.

MARK: He's a *very* good friend.

JEROME: Mark, I'm gay.

MARK: You can't be gay.

JEROME: Why not?

MARK: Because our father isn't henpecked and our mother isn't castrating.

JEROME: I'm still gay.

MARK: What makes you think you're gay?

JEROME: Well, for one thing, I'm extremely enamored with the male form.

MARK: So you have a heightened sense of aesthetics.

JEROME: I also have a lover named Louie.

MARK: Are you sure you're not just doing this to be trendy?

JEROME: Mark, I'm a homosexual.

MARK: Well, I'm stunned. I'm really stunned.

JEROME: I —

MARK: I never even knew you were sexual.

JEROME: Of course, I'm sexual.

MARK: Well, I thought, since the accident...

JEROME: Only my legs went limp; nothing in between... I'm one of the lucky ones.

MARK: You mean, you really can, uh —

JEROME: Uh-huh.

MARK: Really?

JEROME: Yes.

MARK: Really?

JEROME: Well, it does take me longer to climax, but I've never gotten any complaints about that.

MARK: Well... what do you know.

JEROME: To be honest, after the accident, I wasn't sure what I'd be able to do. At the rehab center, they didn't deal with our sexuality at all. At all. Then about six months later, I — I was

JEROME: [*Cont'd.*] watching this Mel Gibson movie, and he started getting real sweaty, and inside I started getting real excited, and outside I got real excited, too.

MARK: Mel Gibson?

JEROME: I know you're shocked that I'm turned on by Mel Gibson. [*Lightly.*] But then, I'm shocked when I meet someone who isn't.

MARK: You're just doing this to be different, aren't you?

JEROME: No.

MARK: Isn't it enough that —

JEROME: Stop it! Look, I, I . . . I know you have trouble accepting things sometimes.

MARK: Like what?

JEROME: Like after the accident, when you visited from college and you offered me a hundred bucks if I took five steps.

MARK: I thought you needed encouragement.

JEROME: My spinal cord had been severed, Mark.

MARK: I know.

JEROME: It was physically impossible.

MARK: Miracles do happen, Jerome!

JEROME: That's exactly what I thought during the Mel Gibson movie.

MARK: Look, I just thought you needed a little push to get better.

JEROME: I was getting better.

MARK: Well, you know, the way the whole family was coddling you; Mom and Grandma were so glad you were alive, they weren't going to ask anything of you.

JEROME: Well, you know, c'mon, they were devastated.

MARK: I didn't want you to get too . . . comfortable.

JEROME: That wasn't likely.

MARK: I didn't see anybody pushing you to get better.

JEROME: You almost made me think —

MARK: Everyone always coddled you.

JEROME: Dad never coddled me.

MARK: Dad never knew either of us existed.

[*This stops the conversation for a moment.*]

JEROME: You're right.

MARK: Look, about this, this deciding to be gay thing, I . . . well, I just can't say I approve.

JEROME: Well then, I guess I'll just have to stop. Next time my pecker rises during a Mel Gibson movie, I'll have to say, "Stop that. Wait till Sharon Stone comes on the screen."

MARK: This doesn't sit right with me, that's all. It just doesn't.

JEROME: Do you want to pretend I never said it?

MARK: This doesn't sit right, that's all. Maybe by your friends it does, but, but not by me.

JEROME: Oh.

MARK: You always get these ideas in your head and, and everyone coddles you . . .

JEROME: Look . . .

MARK: It's not healthy.

JEROME: Mark —

MARK: So I'm giving you a choice.

JEROME: What?!

MARK: I'm giving you a choice.

JEROME: What?

MARK: You can be gay or disabled, but not both.

JEROME: But I *am* both!

MARK: Why can't you be satisfied just being disabled?

JEROME: I don't know. Maybe I'm just selfish.

MARK: Have you considered seeing a shrink about this?

JEROME: I've seen a shrink.

MARK: And what did he say?

JEROME: He said I should accept myself for who I am and stop worrying about whether or not I can please my older brother.

MARK: That sounds like something a shrink would say. Does the school know about this?

JEROME: I'm sure some people suspect, but no.

MARK: 'Cause I'm sure a lot of parents would get pretty upset.

JEROME: I know. Some of them are already nervous about me. I think they're afraid that with me as a role model, some of their kids will want to grow up to be disabled.

MARK: You never used to have this edge.

JEROME: I never used to live in the real world.

MARK: Look, Jerome, about this uh — you sure this isn't just another phase you're going through, you know, like when you were eight and you were positive you wanted to become an astronaut?

JEROME: I don't think —

MARK: You were very serious about it. You had pictures of constellations up on your walls and everything.

JEROME: It's not the same.

MARK: Maybe you think women won't be attracted to you because . . . you know.

JEROME: Mark, I've been with women. I wasn't attracted to them the way I am with men.

MARK: What do you mean, "been with?"

JEROME: I mean everything you think I could mean.

MARK: Even, uh...

JEROME: Uh-huh.

MARK: Were these women ... you know?

JEROME: Hookers?

MARK: No! ... You know.

JEROME: Virgins?

MARK: No.

JEROME: Disabled?

MARK: Yeah.

JEROME: Some were, and some weren't.

MARK: Where'd you meet 'em?

JEROME: Oh, I don't know. School, bars, the post office.

MARK: You picked up girls at the post office?

JEROME: Oh, sure. [*To an imaginary woman.*]"Here, let me hold your package in my lap ... No, it's no effort at all." [JEROME *gives the imaginary woman a big smile.*]

MARK: So then women find you attractive.

JEROME: Well, not an uncontrollable number ...

MARK: And you've had sex with them.

JEROME: Some of them.

MARK: Well, that proves it. You're attracted to women.

JEROME: No! I, uh, the women were, oh, I don't know. I guess, I guess they were an experiment. I mean, I thought I might be gay even before the accident; actually, I was pretty sure of it. Still, I kept thinking, "Maybe if I meet the right woman . . ." Hell, most of the time the only way I could get it up with them was if I fantasized I was with —

MARK: I know. Mel Gibson.

JEROME: Or Tom Cruise.

MARK: You know, both of those men are straight.

JEROME: I don't hold it against them.

MARK: Why do you have this obsession about seducing straight men?

JEROME: I don't have an obsession about seducing straight men. Louie does, but I don't.

MARK: Then he must think you're straight.

JEROME: He doesn't think I'm —

MARK: Well, you said —

JEROME: I just meant —

MARK: If you're not sure —

JEROME: I'm sure —

MARK: You don't sound sure.

JEROME: Mark!

MARK: Why can't you just be disabled?!

JEROME: Look, damn it, I'm disabled and I'm gay, and that's the way it is, whether you like it or not or I like it or not or anybody in the world likes it or not. I didn't ask to be either. I always figured I'd get married someday and I'd walk down the aisle, and surprise, I'm not going to do either. I know I should be proud that I'm gay, and accepting that I'm disabled, and I suppose I am, but damn it, I've sure had to give up a lot of fantasies, a whole truckload of fantasies.

MARK: Look, if you've decided to be gay, that's your decision. I —

JEROME: Oh, yes. That's what it was, a decision. One morning I woke up and thought, "I wonder what I'll do today. See a movie? Go shopping? Turn homo? That sounds interesting."

MARK: Look, I'm sorry, I know this must be hard for you, but I just can't approve.

JEROME: I'm not asking you to approve; I'm asking you to, to accept.

MARK: Well, I'm not sure I can.

JEROME: Why, because I can't be who you want me to be?

MARK: What?

JEROME: It's like when you offered me that money to walk again. I think about that a lot. Was that for me or for you?

MARK: What do you mean?

JEROME: If I could walk again, then you wouldn't have to face the fact that I couldn't.

MARK: I was just trying to help.

JEROME: You or me?

MARK: Damn it, it wasn't my fault you hurt yourself. Just because I had a motorcycle, you didn't have to borrow the neighbors'.

JEROME: That's not why I —

MARK: I didn't do anything wrong.

JEROME: I'm not saying you did.

MARK: I was trying to help.

JEROME: [a surrender, not an agreement] I know.

MARK: Look, Jerome, it's, you know, I'm sure you don't approve of everything I do —

JEROME: I don't want your approval, Mark.

MARK: I mean, I'm sure all your friends think this is perfectly —

JEROME: I don't need your approval.

MARK: Then why did you tell me?!

JEROME: Because you're, you're my brother.

MARK: I know, but —

JEROME: Because you let me tag along with you when you went to get ice cream. Because you explained long division to me

JEROME: [*Cont'd*] better than my teacher. Because you taught me how to play catch.

MARK: You threw like a girl.

JEROME: I don't think it was a sign.

MARK: You know, you could've given me a little hint along the way or something.

JEROME: Like what?

MARK: I don't know. You could've had copies of *Playgirl* lying around.

JEROME: I prefer *Gentleman's Quarterly*. I enjoy mentally disrobing them.

MARK: [*Uncomfortable.*] Really?

JEROME: What?

MARK: Well, I pick up *GQ* at the newsstand sometimes, and it never occurred to me that people might think —

JEROME: Don't worry, Mark. I'm sure lots of heterosexuals read *GQ*. Hundreds maybe.

MARK: You don't act very gay.

JEROME: I'm sorry. Would you like me to wax eloquent about Barbra Streisand?

MARK: I love Streisand.

JEROME: Uh-oh, be careful. First *GQ*, now this.

MARK: I'm not worried about me.

JEROME: Do you ever refer to another guy as "that bitch"?

MARK: It's just, it's a scary time.

JEROME: I'm careful. We're careful.

MARK: Still —

JEROME: You sure you wouldn't like one piece of — [*One of* JEROME'*s legs starts to spasm. It's not significant, but it's noticeable, and it lasts ten to fifteen seconds.*] Uhp, there goes Old Faithful.

MARK: I thought you were taking medication —

JEROME: I stopped years ago. I'm used to them; they don't bother me.

MARK: [*Overlapping a bit.*] Do you ever get spasms at school?

JEROME: Oh, sure. Not often.

MARK: How did the kids react?

JEROME: Oh, the first time, they were freaked out. Then I told them that whoever got the highest mark on the division quiz would get to ride me next time it happened. They got used to it after that.

MARK: You have a lot of guts, Jerome.

JEROME: I just do what I have to do, that's all.

MARK: So why do you think you turned out gay?

JEROME: I don't know. Why do you think you turned out straight?

MARK: I don't know. Jay Wertheimer, remember him?

JEROME: Yeah.

MARK: Jay and I used to sneak looks at his dad's *Playboys* when we were in junior high. Maybe if you had had some experiences like that...

JEROME: Will you stop being so damn superficial?!

MARK: Hey, if I have to accept you're gay, you're going to have to accept I'm superficial. I don't examine things like you do.

JEROME Do you know what Socrates said about the unexamined life?

MARK: It's easier on the nerves?

JEROME: Mark....

MARK: Look, Jerome, the only magazine I read regularly is *People*, and that's only because I fly a lot. My main source of news is the car radio, and half the time I'll switch stations. I work hard, and I don't bother anyone. I may not be a great role model, but nobody's asked me to be.

JEROME: Well, I'm sorry if I'm bothering you with my news.

MARK: You don't have any more surprises for me tonight, do you? You haven't joined a religious cult or anything. You're not a gay disabled Moonie, are you?

JEROME: And if I were?!

MARK: I don't know!

JEROME: Look, I, I...I know this must be hard on you...

MARK: Well, you know, it's like one moment you think the universe is one way; the next moment, it's another way.

JEROME: No, the universe is always the same. The only thing that changes is what you know about it.

MARK: This Louie guy, is he, you know ...

JEROME: An Episcopalian?

MARK: No Is he, you know ...

JEROME: Handicapped? Crippled? Physically challenged? Lame? Euphemism of the month?

MARK: I don't know why you're so angry.

JEROME: It's because I'm afraid that if I ever turn into one of those "nice" cripples, I'll end up on a Jerry Lewis telethon.

MARK: Hey.

JEROME: No, Louie's not disabled.

MARK: How'd you meet?

JEROME: At a gay bake sale. He bought one of my cookies, and then he came back and bought another, and then he came back and bought five more. You know, what they say about the quickest way to man's heart is absolutely true.

MARK: Is that why you took up cooking?

JEROME: No. I took it up because I like to eat.

MARK: Look, I, I'm sorry, I really gotta go.

JEROME: Right.

MARK: If you want, we can discuss it again —

JEROME: Yeah.

MARK: Look, you're going to do whatever you want anyway. You always did.

JEROME: I'm not your little brother anymore, Mark. There's nothing you have to protect me from.

MARK: From what I've read —

JEROME: Let's just drop it, okay?

[*MARK gets ready to go.*]

MARK: Look, dinner was delicious. I won't tell Mom; she'll feel threatened.

JEROME: Goodbye.

MARK: You know, this is a real burden you're laying on me. A real burden.

[JEROME *just looks at* MARK.]

MARK: [Cont'd.] You're asking me for more than I can give. You've always done that. You want me to make everything okay.

JEROME: I don't —

MARK: You wanted the bribe to work. You wanted me to be right. When you were laying in that bed, and everyone else was crying and going nuts, you looked at me, and maybe you don't

MARK: [*Cont'd*] remember, but God, you really wanted someone to believe you could walk. I didn't think you could either, but if you wanted me to think you could, I was willing to play that role.

JEROME: You didn't think —

MARK: Hell, no.

JEROME: I didn't know.

MARK: Older brothers don't give out all their secrets.

JEROME: Any other secrets you kept from me?

MARK: Yeah. I hated it when you tagged along with me to get ice cream.

JEROME: I'm sorry.

MARK: It's okay. It's just that you always insisted on getting a double cone, and halfway through the first scoop there'd be this lava flow coming down your arm.

JEROME: Thanks for cleaning it up.

MARK: Hey, what are older brothers for?

JEROME: Good question.

MARK: Does anyone else in the family know you're —

JEROME: No, I thought I'd try it out on you first.

MARK: So how'd I do?

JEROME: You were — . . . [*Starts to cry.*] I . . . Shit.

MARK: Jerome...

JEROME: I'm sorry, I...

MARK: Hey, you don't have to —

JEROME: I wanted to look so together tonight.

MARK: Hey —

JEROME: I just wanted — shit, shit.

MARK: Calm down.

JEROME: I...I lied.

MARK: You're not gay?

JEROME: No, I mean, yes, I'm gay. I lied about...Yes, damn it, I, I want your approval, and I want your acceptance, and your love, and maybe I'm stupid, maybe I'm stupid for wanting so much from you...Consider it a disability.

MARK: Look, Jerome...

JEROME: I'm just so sick of pretending. I'm so tired of Aunt Debbie always asking me when I'm going to meet that special person. Damn it, I've met that special person.

MARK: Well, you know, Aunt Debbie —

JEROME: I mean, I have a pretty good life, and I know it. But sometimes, I...Sometimes I don't know where to put my sorrow.

MARK: I...I don't know what to say. I don't know what you want me to say.

JEROME: Say you'll stay five minutes and have a piece of my damn pie!

[MARK *looks at* JEROME *a moment.*]

MARK: Okay if I stay five minutes and have a piece of your damn pie?

JEROME: Well, since you asked.

[JEROME *brings the pie to the table. It's beautiful.*]

MARK: You really made that from scratch, huh?

JEROME: That's right.

MARK: Look, you know, I, I'm not sure when I'll be in town next...

JEROME: That's okay. You don't have to —

MARK: It's just that, I don't know, it's —

JEROME: I understand.

MARK: I just want to see what we've got here.

JEROME: Mark —

MARK: So you've really had sex with women...

JEROME: Yes.

MARK: You've had sex with disabled women...

JEROME: Uh-huh.

MARK: And with non-disabled women . . .

JEROME: Uh-huh.

MARK: And with disabled men...

JEROME: That's right.

MARK: And non-disabled men.

JEROME: Yep.

MARK: So the bottom line is . . . you've probably had more sex than I have.

JEROME: It wasn't intentional.

MARK: Well, I just don't think it's right. I'm your older brother, damn it!

JEROME: I'm sorry if I broke the rules.

[MARK *eats a bite of* JEROME'*s pie.*]

MARK: Mmm, this is delicious.

JEROME: I'm a damn good cook, Mark . . . You'll just have to accept that.

[MARK *and* JEROME *look at each other.*]

THE END

Jacquelyn Reingold

TUNNEL OF LOVE

Tunnel of Love by Jacquelyn Reingold. Copyright © 1997 by Jacquelyn Reingold. Reprinted by permission of the Gersh Agency.

Caution: Professionals and amateurs are hereby warned that *Tunnel of Love* is subject to a royalty. It is fully protected under the copyright laws of the United States of America, and of all countries covered by the Pan-America Copyright Convention and the Universal Copyright Convention, and of all countries with which the United States has reciprocal copyright relations. All rights, including professional, amateur, motion picture, recitation, lecturing, public reading, radio broadcasting, television, video or sound taping, all other forms of mechanical or electronic reproduction, such as information storage and retrieval systems and photocopying, and the rights of translation into foreign languages, are strictly reserved. Particular emphasis is laid upon the question of readings, permission for which must be secured from the author's agent in writing.

All inquiries concerning rights should be addressed to Scott Yoselow, c/o The Gersh Agency, 130 West 42nd St., New York, New York 10036.

Jacquelyn Reingold

Jacquelyn Reingold's play, *Girl Gone*, was produced off-Broadway by the MCC Theatre, and then in 1996 at the City Garage in Los Angeles. It received the Kennedy Center's Fund for New American Plays Roger Stevens Award, and is published in *Women Playwrights: The Best Plays of 1994*. Her one-act, *Dear Kenneth Blake*, was produced in Ensemble Studio Theatre's Marathon '94, and by Theatre Geo in Los Angeles in 1997, where it won a Dramalogue Award in Playwriting. It is published in *The Best American Short Plays 1994-5*.

Jacquelyn's other plays, which include *Freeze Tag*, *Lost and Found*, *A.M.I.*, *Joe and Stew*, and *Creative Development*, have been seen in New York at Ensemble Studio Theatre, Naked Angels, MCC, Primary Stages, the Working Theatre, the Circle Rep Lab, as well as at theatres across the country and in London. Her work has been published by Dramatists Play Service, Samuel French, Smith and Kraus, and in *The Quarterly*. She has written and directed plays for inner city kids at the 52nd Street Project, and is a member playwright of New Dramatists and Ensemble Studio Theatre.

Tunnel of Love was first workshopped at Naked Angels, directed by Ethan Siverman, and acted by Kimberly Flynn, Susan Greenhill, Merrill Holtzman, Karen Kandel, Martha Plimpton, and Tisha Roth. It was first produced in Ensemble Studio Theatre's Marathon '93, directed by Ethan Silverman, and acted by Amelia Campbell, Bill Cwikowski, David Eigenberg, Christine Farrell, Karen Kandel, and Angela Pietropinto. It was produced in 1996 at Theatre of NOTE in Los Angeles where it received a Dramalogue Award in Playwriting, and in 1997 at the Shadowbox Theatre in Columbus, Ohio.

CHARACTERS

SUSIE   Quirky, confused, trying to cope as the world spins around her. Wears an oversized "Laura Ashley"-type dress. In her early 20s.

GARY   A guy guy. Trying hard to do his best. In his 20s.

DOCTOR CHECKUP

DOCTOR MUFFIN

DOCTOR BEAVER

DOCTOR SNATCH

DOCTOR TOO-LIPS

JO

FIFI

THERESA

WOMAN 1

WOMAN 2

WOMAN 3

WOMAN 4

TIME: Now.

NOTE: An ensemble of 3 women and one man play all roles except SUSIE and GARY. Also, there are no blackouts between scenes.

SCENE 1

Doctor's office. SUSIE *sits in a tiny child sized chair.* DOCTOR CHECKUP *sits in a large chair. He looks very big. On his chest is a name-tag that reads, "Dr. Anton Checkup." He has a Russian accent.*

DOCTOR CHECKUP: So. I'm Dr. Anton Checkup. And you're — [*He looks at a paper.*] Susie. So. Any aches and pains?

SUSIE: No.

DOCTOR CHECKUP: Ongoing childhood diseases?

SUSIE: No.

DOCTOR CHECKUP: Shortness of breath?

SUSIE: No.

DOCTOR CHECKUP: Runny nose?

SUSIE: No.

DOCTOR CHECKUP: Post-feminist depression?

SUSIE: No.

DOCTOR CHECKUP: Tummy ache?

SUSIE: No.

DOCTOR CHECKUP: Heartache?

SUSIE: Um, well, no.

DOCTOR CHECKUP: Problems with peeing or pooping?

SUSIE: No.

DOCTOR CHECKUP: Exercise?

SUSIE: Stairmaster.

DOCTOR CHECKUP: Ulcer due to backlash anger?

SUSIE: No.

DOCTOR CHECKUP: Eyes? [SUSIE *points to her eyes.*] Ears? [*She points to ears.*] Nose? [*She points to nose.*]

DOCTOR CHECKUP: Married?

SUSIE: No.

DOCTOR CHECKUP: In a relationship?

SUSIE: Uh, no. I was, but he um, just left me.

DOCTOR CHECKUP: [*He looks at her.*] Anorgasmic or orgasmic?

SUSIE: Excuse me?

DOCTOR CHECKUP: Have you had one or haven't you?

SUSIE: Umm.

DOCTOR CHECKUP: Hmm. And no trouble peeing or pooping.

SUSIE: No.

DOCTOR CHECKUP: My wife's a social worker, I recommend

DOCTOR CHECKUP: [*Cont'd.*] counseling. Otherwise, you're healthy. Come back next year. Find a man. Pay 600 dollar bill at desk.

SUSIE: Wait.

DOCTOR CHECKUP: Yes?

SUSIE: I do have a problem.

DOCTOR CHECKUP: Yes.

SUSIE: With.

DOCTOR CHECKUP: Yes?

SUSIE: My.

DOCTOR CHECKUP: Yes? [*She crosses to him and stands on tiptoe to whisper in his ear.*] Oh. Go on. [*She whispers.*] Interesting. I'd like to have a look at that.

SCENE 2

Phone call. GARY *in his apartment, fixing something with his tools.* SUSIE *at home.*

SUSIE: Gary?

GARY: Yeah?

SUSIE: Hi, it's Susie.

GARY: Oh, hi. Hang on. [*He uses his screwdriver.*]

SUSIE: What are you doing?

GARY: Fixing objects so that I can feel like I have infinite power over my world.

SUSIE: Nice.

GARY: Sorry things didn't work out with us. I just couldn't handle it. I mean, I still can't. I mean, let's cut to the chase here. Why are you calling?

SUSIE: I just wanted to say that—[*He drops something.*] What are you doing?

GARY: Breaking things so that I can fix them so that I can feel like I have infinite power over my world.

SUSIE: Oh. Well, I went to the doctor.

GARY: Good. It's good to take action.

SUSIE: You were right.

GARY: It's good to be right. Tough break for you, though.

SUSIE: Well, the doctor said there was hope.

GARY: Oh? You mean like a repair job?

SUSIE: And I was wondering, if they can, you know—

GARY: I see—would I want to be a couple—movies, dinner, nesting, that sort of thing.

SUSIE: The doctor recommended it.

GARY: Look, uh, my, my phone is ringing.

SUSIE: It is?

GARY: I mean, the door is ringing.

SUSIE: I have an appointment with a specialist.

GARY: Hey, well, like, I don't know, I mean, yours seemed like a problem even I couldn't fix. So, let me know what happens, if you get it worked out or worked in or whatever, Susie. You're a sweetheart. Gotta go. [*He exits.*]

SCENE 3

Another Doctor's office. SUSIE *sits on her little chair, or on a table with wheels.* DOCTOR MUFFIN *appears.*

DOCTOR MUFFIN: I'm Dr. Muffin.

SUSIE: Hi, Dr. Checkup gave me your name. I was—

DOCTOR MUFFIN: Oh, yes. Mind if I take a look?

[SUSIE *spreads her legs.* DOCTOR BEAVER *appears.*]

DOCTOR BEAVER: I'm Dr. Beaver.

DOCTOR MUFFIN: Interesting.

SUSIE: Hi, Dr. Muffin gave me your name. I was wondering—

DOCTOR BEAVER: Interesting. Mind if I take a look?

[DOCTOR SNATCH *appears.*]

DOCTOR SNATCH: I'm Dr. Snatch.

SUSIE: Dr. um, Beaver gave me your name. I was wondering if—

DOCTOR MUFFIN: So, you growing potatoes in there?

SUSIE: What?

DOCTOR BEAVER: Are you married?

SUSIE: No.

DOCTOR SNATCH: Oh, yes, Mind if I —

SUSIE: — take a look?

DOCTOR BEAVER: In a relationship?

DOCTOR MUFFIN: Post feminist depression?

SUSIE: Ooh.

DOCTOR SNATCH: Interesting.

DOCTOR BEAVER: Are you seeing a psychiatrist?

SUSIE: Ow.

DOCTOR MUFFIN: Do you mind it when men sit with their legs spread apart?

DOCTOR BEAVER: My cousin's an analyst.

DOCTOR SNATCH: I'd like to take a look.

DOCTOR MUFFIN: I like to look.

SUSIE: Doctor, do you think—?

DOCTOR MUFFIN: Let me call in my partners.

[DOCTOR TOO-LIPS *apppears.*]

DOCTOR TOO-LIPS: I'm Dr. Too-Lips.

DOCTOR BEAVER: Get the camera.

SUSIE: Hey.

[SUSIE *is spun around and/or pulled around the stage. Or perhaps it's just the* DOCTORS *that are moving. At some point strange, large, examining instruments appear.*]

DOCTOR MUFFIN: I think there's someone else I'd like you to see.

DOCTOR TOO-LIPS: Do you have a boyfriend?

DOCTOR BEAVER: I think I'd like to see.

DOCTOR TOO-LIPS: Do you have a friend?

DOCTOR SNATCH: I'd like you to come back.

DOCTOR BEAVER: We think it can be fixed.

DOCTOR TOO-LIPS: Do you know any men?

SUSIE: Hey!!

DOCTOR MUFFIN: Interesting.

DOCTOR SNATCH: I can't see.

DOCTOR BEAVER: Let me look.

DOCTOR TOO-LIPS: I'd like to see.

[DOCTORS *in a circle around* SUSIE, *passing the instruments to each other. Fast.*]

DOCTOR MUFFIN, DOCTOR BEAVER, DOCTOR SNATCH, & DOCTOR TOO-LIPS: I can't see ... Let me look ... Interesting ... Do you have a ... Interesting ... I'd like to see ... I can't see .. boyfriend? ... Do ... I can't see ... Let me look ... Interesting ... you have a Interesting ... I'd like to see ... I can't see ... friend? ... Do you ... I can't see ... Let me look ... Interesting ... have a boy- Interesting ... I'd like to see ... I can't see ... friend? ... Do you?

DOCTORS: I'd like to take a look. [*They aim the instruments at her.*]

SCENE 4

Support Group. WOMEN *drink from styrofoam coffee cups. The scene should start realistically, in chairs, then move into a heightened, presentational staging, and then back to chairs.*

JO: Hi, my name is Jo.

GROUP: Hi, Jo. [*Applause.*]

FIFI: Hi, my name is Fifi.

GROUP: Hi, Fifi. [*Applause.*]

THERESA: I'm Theresa.

GROUP: Hi, Theresa. [*Applause.*]

THERESA: I didn't know 'til I was married.

JO: I thought my life was ruined.

FIFI: My life was over.

THERESA: I'd never really looked.

JO: It looked normal from the outside.

THERESA: My husband was surprised.

FIFI: I read about it in Cosmo. [*Holds up* Cosmopolitan *magazine.*]

JO: They wrote about it in Cosmo. [*Holds up* Cosmopolitan *magazine.*]

THERESA: We read about it in Cosmo. [*Holds up* Cosmopolitan *magazine.*]

GROUP: [*Reading from* Cosmo.] Sometimes nature slips up.

JO: Cleft palate—

THERESA: —harelip—

FIFI: —clubfoot—

JO: —but there is one abnormality few of us have heard of.

GROUP: Yet today, there are twenty to thirty thousand women, like us, in the U.S. alone who were born with: CAV.

THERESA: [*Not from* Cosmo.] I found out on my wedding night. We were in Bermuda. I was still a virgin.

FIFI: [*Not from* Cosmo.] I found out as a teen ager. You know, on my own.

JO: [*Not from* Cosmo.] I found out at the doctor.

THERESA: My husband was unable to penetrate. Much to our displeasure.

FIFI: I knew right away something was wrong.

THERESA: For months I was still a virgin.

JO: I was having an examination. He called in his partners.

GROUP: We were diagnosed with C.A.V.

THERESA: Congenital—

FIFI: — absence —

JO: — of —

THERESA: — the —

GROUP: [*Loud whisper to* SUSIE.] — vagina.

THERESA: I became hysterical.

FIFI: I felt like I wasn't a woman.

JO: I was a freak.

THERESA: I had surgery as fast as possible.

[*Overlapping section:*]

FIFI: [*Reads from* Cosmo.] Skin from the buttocks is wrapped around a mold, held in place by suturing. Fourteen days later the mold is removed.

JO: [*Reads.*] Nature, unfortunately, recognizing the opening as foreign, wants to close it down.

THERESA: [*Reads.*] A patient must keep it open with frequent coitus or by using dilators regularly.

[*Overlapping ends.*]

GROUP: [*Reads.*] One day a doctor heard of a woman who created hers through coitus, and it didn't close down.

JO: He thought it would be possible—

FIFI: —to create a neo vagina without surgery—

THERESA: —and he began experimenting.

JO: He had a—

FIFI: —patient sit on—

THERESA: —a stool with—

JO: —a lucite—

FIFI: —dilator fo—

THERESA: —15 to—

JO: —30 minutes—

FIFI: —a day.

JO: It—

THERESA: —involved—

FIFI: —time—

JO: —patience—

THERESA: —and—

FIFI: —motivation—

GROUP: —but it worked.

GROUP & SUSIE: Once CAV was a devastating diagnosis for any young girl. But today, women, like us, can lead satisfying, sexually active lives.

THERESA: I had the surgery. You have to keep it in use. My husband loves it.

FIFI: I used the stool.

JO: I had the surgery, then it closed, then I used the stool.

THERESA: I'm a changed woman.

JO: I stare at skyscrapers.

FIFI: My husband really loves me now.

THERESA: I like to keep objects inside of mine.

JO: I was afraid after my first one closed down.

THERESA: Spare change, my keys, date book. Things I don't want to misplace.

JO: My boyfriend was very supportive. He loves it.

FIFI: They love it.

GROUP: Your boyfriend will love it.

SCENE 5

Phone call. GARY *with money, a computer, calculator; wearing athletic/career clothes. Loud sounds of TV sports.*

SUSIE: Gary, it's Susie.

GARY: Oh hi. [*He catches a football.*]

SUSIE: What are you doing?

GARY: [*He counts money.*] I'm keeping very busy with external activities so I don't have to experience any inner feelings.

SUSIE: Oh.

GARY: [*He works on a computer.*] You know sports, cars, sex, money, career advancement. I'm very busy, not much time to talk.

SUSIE: I see.

GARY: [*He watches a game on TV, yells at the set.*] Pass! Run! Jump! GO!

SUSIE: Well I just wanted to let you know I'm getting one.

GARY: Oh? [*He pulls out the tv remote. Silence*]

SUSIE: It should be ready in a while. I think you'll love it. I'll be a virgin, Gary.

GARY: [*With reverence, he puts on a baseball cap. A baseball bat appears, he takes it.*] Give me the chance, I'll hit a home run.

SUSIE: Yeah?

GARY: Let me know when it's opening day. [*He swings the bat.*]

SCENE 6

Doctor's waiting room. Sexy looking women sit.

WOMAN 1: I'm having my breasts enlarged.

WOMAN 2: I'm having mine reduced.

WOMAN 4: I'm having my lips inflated.

WOMAN 3: I'm having my hips deflated.

WOMAN 4: Collagen injection.

WOMAN 2: Silicone rejection.

WOMAN 3: Nipple lift.

WOMAN 4: This is my fifth.

WOMAN 1: Chemical peel.

WOMAN 3: Cheeks revealed.

WOMAN 1: Liposuction.

WOMAN 2: Bulge reduction.

WOMAN 4: Ribs removed.

WOMAN 3: Jaw—

WOMAN 2: —reimproved.

> [ALL *look at* SUSIE.]

SUSIE: [*Whispers.*] Vagina. [*Full voice.*] I'm getting a [*Whispers.*] vagina.

WOMAN 2: Really?

WOMAN 3: Wow.

WOMAN 4: A new one?

WOMAN 1: I never thought of that.

SCENE 7

> *Phone call.* GARY *is drumming.*

SUSIE: Hi, it's Susie. What are you doing?

GARY: Drumming. I'm reading that revolutionary "pumping iron in the john" book. [*He drums.*] My name is Gary, son of Barry.

SUSIE: I wanted to give you an update.

GARY: [*Stops drumming.*] I'm finding my manhood. If you're gonna talk about—about, I mean, women's parts and — eew — you know — eew.

SUSIE: Well, I'm in the middle of a session. I've been sitting here. Expanding. And, Gary, do you want to know what I think about?

GARY: What?

SUSIE: Sometimes I think about you. [*He turns to her.*] And, Gary. It's beginning to work.

GARY: It is?

[*He drums with enthusiasm.*]

SCENE 8

Support group.

SUSIE: It's beginning to work.

GROUP: How do you feel?

SUSIE: Different.

JO, THERESA, and FIFI: Yes? ... I knew it ... I told you.

SUSIE: I have   I have this yearning feeling

JO, THERESA, and FIFI: Oh yes, oh yes ... Oh really? ... Tell us.

SUSIE: Like I need to nurture someone.

JO: Try volunteering.

SUSIE: And an interest in children.

FIFI: I bought a puppy.

SUSIE: And a need to relate to other relationships.

THERESA: Try the afternoon talk shows.

SUSIE: And at the same time I feel angry. I see, I see injustice and sexism and it makes me angry. It's confusing. Things are getting very confused.

FIFI: Oh, that.

JO: Being a woman.

THERESA: Try therapy.

JO: Oh, yes.

FIFI: Being a woman.

THERESA: Counseling.

JO: Oh, that.

FIFI: That.

GROUP: Oh, *that*.

SCENE 9

SUSIE *alone. Almost like a nursery rhyme.*

SUSIE: The Freudian said penis envy. A Jungian, animus fear. Psychiatrist said chemical imbalance. Psychopharmacologist thought Prozac needed here. The psychic said the answer is the future; psychologist, the future's in the past, don't fear. Internist called a gynecologist, support group says—

[SUPPORT GROUP *appears.*]

GROUP: Just keep stretching it, Dear! [GROUP *exits.*]

SCENE 10

[SUSIE, *alone.*]

SUSIE: Oh my God. I have, I have, this empty feeling. I feel so, so, empty. I want to find fulfillment. I want to fill this empty feeling. I want to be pretty. I have to help others. I want to wear silk teddies and push-up bras. I want men to open the door for me and then I want to say "Do I look like I have no arms?" I want to go dancing in high heels and let men lead, and then I get mad when they don't know the steps and I'm not supposed to show them. I want men to notice me and then I want to punch them when they stare. I want to feed children in the third world and scream at the white male cold war politicians who sent the guns there and screwed it up in the first place. I want to shoot guns at truck drivers and bomb operation rescue. I want men to give me a seat on the subway and I want to tell

SUSIE: [*Cont'd.*] the one next to me to stop taking up so much room, why don't you close your legs, what have you got between them, an aircraft carrier?! I want to lash back at the backlash. I have a hole inside me now. All of this because of a hole?

SCENE 11

GARY *dials the phone. He takes a deflated blow up doll out of a box.* SUSIE *picks up.*

GARY: Susie.

SUSIE: Hi.

GARY: Listen, I'm—I'm, uh, practicing for the big day, you know, exercises, technique, defining goals to make sure we achieve them, you know, win the gold medal, blue ribbon, first place, one for the gipper.

SUSIE: Gary, you make me really angry.

GARY: Oh. [*He drops the doll.*]

SUSIE: I—I want to hurt you.

GARY: Well, then, I—I want to get away from you.

SUSIE: I wouldn't nurture you if you were the last human on earth.

GARY: I wouldn't get near you with a ten foot pole.

SUSIE: Well your testicles are hairy!

GARY: And your vagina is — missing!

SUSIE: [*She talks directly to him.*] Not anymore.

GARY: [*He talks directly to her.*] It isn't?

SUSIE: No.

GARY: Can I come over?

SUSIE: I'm wearing crotchless panties.

GARY: I'll be right there. [*He exits.*]

SCENE 12

[SUSIE *unbuttons her two top buttons and puts on lipstick.* GARY *enters wearing a test pilot outfit.*]

SUSIE: Hi.

GARY: Hi, Sexy. You ready?

SUSIE: What are you wearing?

GARY: Test pilot, ready for take off.

SUSIE: Gary, before we go any further, I just have to tell you—

GARY: Go where no man has gone before.

SUSIE: That I think you're a jerk.

GARY: Can I touch it now?

SUSIE: And a pig.

GARY: Oink oink. Now can I?

SUSIE: The way you dumped me then and the way you want me now.

GARY: Come on, baby, let's go exploring.

SUSIE: All because of a hole.

GARY: I want to be your Christopher Columbus.

SUSIE: Gary.

GARY: Cortez, Ponce De Leon. Neil Armstrong. Stormin' Norman. [*He puts on the goggles.*]

SUSIE: That does it. I changed my mind.

GARY: What?

SUSIE: I'm not interested, I'm just not interested. It's my vagina. It is. I made it, it's mine — V-A-G-I-N-A. I don't have to share. I can have a satisfying life without sharing it with you. So, no. It's my hole. And if I want to spend my life crawled up inside of it without you or anyone, then I will. And if you don't like it, you can go. If that's all you're here for, leave. Find yourself another hole.

GARY: [*Stunned. Looks at her, confused.*] Well. What about your mouth?

SUSIE: Well, what about the inside of one of your drums? Or why don't you hollow out your baseball bat? I know, just unzip your pants and head for the Holland tunnel. Even better, Gary, use your own hole, the one between your ears, just put your dick in you head and fuck what little you have of your own brains out!

GARY: [*Beat.*] Nice. I'm really glad you've found yourself.

SUSIE: Me too. [*Pause. They stand there.*] So, what are you waiting for? Leave. I'm not the only hole in the universe.

GARY: [*Pause.*] I don't want to leave.

SUSIE: Why not?

GARY: I don't know.

SUSIE: Why did you ever even talk to me in the first place?

GARY: Mmm. Your face. I think. Something about your face. Made me want to say hi. And then, something about what you said.

SUSIE: What did I say?

GARY: "Hi." But it was the way you said it. "Hi." And when I asked if I could see you sometime and you said, "That would be nice," that was nice. I guess I liked you. And, well, I guess I kinda like you feisty even better.

SUSIE: Oh.

GARY: Why did you talk to me?

SUSIE: You had nice buns.

GARY: Yeah?

SUSIE: [*She shrugs.*] I looked at you and I knew I wanted—to wrestle.

GARY: [*Beat.*] Susie. I know I can be a jerk. I couldn't—I didn't know how to—I—Sorry. Look, what if we—what if we just, you know, tried to be, like, close.

SUSIE: What do you mean?

GARY: You know, like, lie down and do the close thing.

SUSIE: What?

GARY: You know, that talking and feeling thing. How would that be?

SUSIE: I don't know.

GARY: Yeah. Forget it.

SUSIE: [*Beat.*] It might be ok.

GARY: Yeah?

SUSIE: Yeah.

GARY: We could try.

SUSIE: We could. Take off the helmet.

> [*He does. Music plays. They take off their shoes as the* ENSEMBLE *enters with sheet and pillows to create a vertical bed. They 'get in bed,' on opposite ends. They, very gingerly and slowly, get close. They sigh. They smile.*]

GARY: So, how is it?

SUSIE: It's — nice. How is it for you?

GARY: Nice.

SUSIE: Gary?

GARY: Yeah?

SUSIE: Do you sit on the subway with your legs spread?

GARY: Yeah.

SUSIE: Why?

GARY: Just born that way, I guess.

SUSIE: Oh.

GARY: I think I'm gonna fall asleep now. Good night.

SUSIE: 'Night.

> [*He snores, then pushes her all the way to the edge of the bed.*]

SUSIE: Gary?

GARY: [*Asleep.*] Huh?

SUSIE: [*With clarity.*] Move over.

[*He rolls over to his edge. They are apart.* SUSIE *reaches out her hand across the bed,* GARY *reaches out his hand. They touch.*]

[*BLACKOUT.*]

THE END

Murray Schisgal

FIFTY YEARS AGO

Fifty Years Ago by Murray Schisgal. Copyright © 1996 by Murray Schisgal. All rights reserved. Reprinted by permission of the author.

CAUTION: Professionals and amateurs are hereby warned that *Fifty Years Ago* by Murray Schisgal is subject to a royalty. It is fully protected under the copyright laws of the United States of America, and of all countries covered by the International Copyright Union (including the Dominion of Canada and the rest of the British Commonwealth), and of all countries covered by the Pan-American Convention and the Universal Copyright Convention, and of all countries with which the United States has reciprocal copyright relations. All rights, including professional, amateur, motion picture, recitation, lecturing, public reading, radio broadcasting, television, video or sound taping, all other forms of mechanical or electronic reproduction, such as information storage and retrieval systems and photocopying, and the rights of translation into foreign languages, are strictly reserved. Particular emphasis is placed upon the question of readings, permission for which must be secured from the author's agent in writing.

All inquiries should be addressed to the author's representative: Arthur B. Greene, 101 Park Avenue, New York, NY 10016.

Murray Schisgal

Murray Schisgal has had six plays produced on Broadway, a good many Off-Broadway, Off-off-Broadway, and in regional and foreign theaters. He was nominated for a Tony for his play *LUV*, an Oscar for co-writing the film *Tootsie* (it won the New York Film Critics, Los Angeles Film Critics, National Society of Film Critics, Writers Guild of America, and Hollywood Foreign Press Association Awards). His original TV screenplay, *The Love Song of Barney Kempinski* won an Emmy Award. His other credits include *The Typists* and *The Tiger*, which received the Outer Circle and Vernon Rice Awards. Twelve of his one-act plays have appeared in various anthologies. *Slouching Towards the Millennium*, three one-act plays, was produced in 1997 at the 42nd Street Workshop.

CHARACTERS

DONALD

PATRICIA

SETTING: *The Lumleys' living-room in a brownstone on West 88th Street, Manhattan.*

TIME: *August 14, 1995. Day*

AT RISE: *Folding chairs have been added to the armchairs and sofa, set in a semi-circle, to accommodate the guests who are coming to a party. Canapés and appetizers are on a silver plate; nuts and potato chips in carnival-glass bowls; bottles of champagne, wine and mineral water on coasters or in ice buckets; etc. Several crepe-paper streamers crisscross overhead. Fresh-cut flowers also decorate the room.*

A door to the bedroom is on the right; a door to the ping-pong room is on the left; the entrance door is upstage, left.
PATRICIA is dressing in the bedroom, DONALD in the ping-pong room. The doors to both rooms are open, but we can't see the occupants.
PATRICIA and DONALD are in their seventies.

DONALD (*Offstage.*): Patty m'girl? [*No response; louder.*] Patty? [*No response; a folding chair is thrown against the wall in the ping-pong room, clattering to the floor.*]

PATRICIA (*Offstage.*): [*In a panic.*] What is it? What was that? Are you all right, Donald? Did you hurt yourself? Did you fall or have an accident? Did you break anything? Talk to me! Talk to me!

DONALD (OS): [*Cool as a cucumber.*] I am perfectly fine.

PATRICIA (OS): Then what was that horrible noise? What in God's name happened?

DONALD (OS): It seems the only way I can get your attention when I speak to you is by making you think I've had an accident or I suffered a debilitating stroke !

PATRICIA (OS): [*Heavily emphatic.*] That is not true. That is blatantly not true!

DONALD (OS): It is! It is absolutely true! I've learned something being married to you for one full year!

PATRICIA (OS): What, may I ask, is it that you've learned?

DONALD: [*Only his head is visible in doorway; he is wearing shower-cap; shouts.*] You're hard of hearing! [*Head retreats back into room.*]

PATRICIA (OS): I am not hard of hearing! I'm preoccupied. I have to get dressed. My focus is on getting dressed, not on being convivial!

DONALD (OS): I don't mean to offend you. And I certainly don't mean to quarrel with you on this very special occasion. But I do recall during my first marriage . . .

PATRICIA: [*Only her head is visible in doorway; her hair is dyed with a reddish hue and is rolled in purple, plastic curlers.*] Don't do this to me, Donald. Please, Please, do not do this to me.

DONALD (OS): [*Heedlessly.*] If I coughed, if I sneezed, if I cracked my knuckles, Bertha was at my side, immediately, with a handkerchief or a band-aid or a glass of alka seltzer!

PATRICIA: [*Rigidly.*] I take it you're talking about the first . . . [*Pinched voice.*] . . . Mrs. Lumley, Mr. Lumley.

DONALD (OS): I am. I cannot, after all those years of living with another woman, disregard my experiences with her. I would merely whisper her name in the bedroom — and she would instantaneously rush in from the garden, an unplanted rhododendron bush still in her hands !

PATRICIA (OS): [*Retreats into bedroom.*] I forbid myself, and I have forbidden myself in the past, to utter a single derogatory word against the first Mrs. Lumley. Is that not so, Mr. Lumley?

DONALD (OS): It is. As is befitting and proper in view of the fact that Bertha is gone from this earthly vale of tears.

PATRICIA: [*Head appears in doorway; no curlers.*] To me, Donald, your first wife, whatever her name might be, is still with us. Literally speaking, she will always be with us.

DONALD: [*Head appears in ping-pong room doorway; shaving cream on his face; no shower-cap.*] That is an oxymoron!

PATRICIA: That is not an oxymoron!

DONALD: How can you explain to me the following: "Literally speaking, she will always be with us."

PATRICIA: Because, my dear husband...May I call you my dear husband?

DONALD: Legally, I cannot prevent it.

PATRICIA: Because, my dear husband, she is constantly about us, in the air we breathe, in the water we drink, in the food we eat. Like a pollutant.

DONALD: Be forewarned. Beee forewarned! You are talking of the mother of my three, *priceless* daughters! [*Retreats from sight.*]

PATRICIA: [*Nodding mournfully.*] How well I know it. Full well do I...[*Suddenly in a panic; shouts.*] Donald, I love you!

DONALD: [*Head in doorway at once; no shaving cream on face.*] And I, you! I, you, my sweet, my treasure, my heart!

PATRICIA: Oh, I float on air. I'm in a land of dreams.

DONALD: Do you remember the vow I took one year this evening in our marital chamber?

PATRICIA: Vividly. Lucidly. As well as I remember the day we first met.

DONALD: Fifty years ago.

PATRICIA: In Manila.

DONALD: In the far reaches of the Pacific.

PATRICIA: On VJ Day.

DONALD: Fifty years ago.

PATRICIA: A twin celebration, my darling. Our first anniversary and the anniversary of the unconditional surrender of the Japanese.

DONALD: Happy days. Happy days. [*Stretches his hand out.*] If only I could touch you.

PATRICIA: [*Stretches her hand out.*] My fingers ache for your fingers.

DONALD: What vow was it, my sweet, that I took in our marital chamber one year this evening? [*They withdraw their hands.*]

PATRICIA: That death itself would not separate us.

DONALD: So shall it be. I vow it again, two-fold, ten-fold, a hundred-fold! And now...Are you ready, Patty m'girl? Are you dressed? Are you made up? Can we begin our party?

PATRICIA: Yes, yes, but... You come out first.

DONALD: I need another minute. You come out first. Please, I beseech you, I beg you. Let's not make an issue of this.

PATRICIA: I'll be magnanimous.

DONALD: As you are inevitably!

PATRICIA: I'll come out first, but you are not to laugh, smirk, smile, grin, or make a single snide or critical remark!

DONALD: I wouldn't. Never. Am I not in the same boat as you are? Am I not susceptible to the same calumnies as you are?

PATRICIA: Keep that firmly in mind. Lastly, you are not to look at me either directly or surreptitiously until I call your name. Agreed?

DONALD: Agreed !

PATRICIA: Return to the ping-pong room, please.

DONALD (OS): [*Retreats.*] I'll finish dressing. Don't take too long. Our guests will be arriving momentarily!

[*PATRICIA looks about, wanting to make certain that there's absolutely no one watching her. Tentatively, timidly, she steps out of the bedroom. She's wearing a WW2 nurse's uniform. It's too small on her, as are the white shoes and cap. She feels miserable.*]

DONALD (OS): [*Cont'd.*] Patty m'girl? [*No response; louder.*] Patty? [*No response; a folding chair is thrown against the wall, clattering to the floor.*]

PATRICIA: [*Almost in tears.*] If you must come out and gape at me, come out and gape at me. I think your idea of how to celebrate our anniversaries is positively ridiculous and infantile and unworthy of a man of your intelligence. I cannot, for the life of me...

[*She stops in mid-speech at the sight of* DONALD *entering. He's wearing his pitifully too small WW2 navy uniform; a wide belt or suspenders hold up his trousers and a white cap is perched at the rear of his head. Two rows of campaign ribbons are on his chest and his left arm has a Radioman 3rd Class insignia. He beams like a poppycock. He feels, and believes he looks, terrific.* PATRICIA, *wide-eyed, raises her finger to point at him; her cheeks blow up and a hawking, throaty laugh erupts from her, building to a howling crescendo.*]

DONALD: [*Perplexed.*] What's funny? [*Is she laughing at him?*] What, may I ask, is so funny?

PATRICIA: [*Interrupted laughter.*] That... That... That... [*Screwing her face in to a somber expression.*] I think you look very attractive in your uniform. [*She has to turn away from him; lips glued together.*]

DONALD: [*Pulls down on blouse.*] All things considered, I'd say we both look very attractive. We put on a few pounds, but it's only natural. It's nothing to be ashamed of. [*Pointing at her.*] You see, Patricia, that's the difference between us. I speak what has to be spoken, objectively, not emotionally. I acknowledge the circumstance, I deal with it, correct it, and go beyond it. That's something you've never learned to do.

PATRICIA: [*Thinks; magnanimously.*] You're right. You're one of the most perceptive and brilliant men I know. My first husband...

DONALD: I prefer we do not discuss your first husband.

PATRICIA: Donny-o, I also do not want us to quarrel on this auspicious occasion. Having said that, however, I will say that I reserve unto myself the inalienable right to talk about my first husband, my inestimable son, and the life I lived prior to our matrimony!

DONALD: [*Glances at wristwatch.*] Talk, talk if you must! But talk fast. Our guests are practically knocking on the door. [*He sits on sofa; picks up a handful of nuts.*]

PATRICIA: [*Sits on chair; pours mineral water.*] Must we go on with this charade? Why can't we just have a nice little celebration,, an intimate *petit dejeuner deux*? We can dance, we can drink champagne, we can enjoy the fruits...

DONALD: Patty m'girl, you have given me your word, your solemn, sworn word that you'd go along with what I deem to be the most momentous anniversaries of our mortal existence. Are you, and I ask you this calmly and unperturbably, are you reneging on your solemnly sworn word?

PATRICIA: [*Thinks; magnanimously.*] No. I am not. I thought I might convince you of an alternative means of celebration. But since I cannot, I will greet our... guests and I will act in an appropriate manner. I do, however, continue to reserve unto myself the inalienable right to talk to our guests as an unfettered, individual entity who also served her country in a time of national crisis. And for the record, let me add, I volunteered of my own free will and volition. I was not drafted as some others I can mention.

DONALD: [*Grievously offended.*] I knew I should never have told you everything about my private life before we were married. I knew it in the deepest recesses of my being. But I said to myself, I'm in love with this woman, there should be no secrets between us; besides, she would never be soooo insensitive, soooo vindictive as to throw it all back in my face in a fit of postmenopausal distemper!

PATRICIA: Be that as it is, may I continue to tell you what I was going to tell you about my first husband?

DONALD: Legally, I do not have the power to stop you.

PATRICIA: Then as I was saying, you, you are one of the most perceptive and brilliant men I know. My first husband, Herman...

[*DONALD cringes at the mention of his name.*]

...being by profession an actuarial statistician was also a perceptive and brilliant man... And I am compelled by maternal instinct to add another name to that honor roll: my son, Jonathan.

DONALD: [*Dubiously.*] Your son, Jonathan, a perceptive and brilliant man.

PATRICIA: Yes.

DONALD: The same Jonathan who has not been employed for the last five years.

PATRICIA: Yes.

DONALD: The same Jonathan who is still without wife at the age of forty-six.

PATRICIA: He's a genius.

DONALD: Jonathan.

PATRICIA: Yes. He's writing an encyclopedia.

DONALD: For whom? For baboons? For... [*Anguished.*] Ohhh, what am I saying. What's wrong with me? [*In a panic; on his knee beside her.*] Patricia, my precious, my sweetheart, my darling, my wife, my reason to get up in the morning, my reason for going to bed at night. I love you, I love you, I do love you!

PATRICIA: And I, you! you! you! Oh, dear, dear Donny-o, where would I be without you! What life would I have? What day or week or month would I have if not for the warmth of you next to me?

DONALD: Let's not ever, ever, ever quarrel again!

PATRICIA: Why do we? What is this insanity? I... like your three daughters.

DONALD: Do you?

PATRICIA: They're... lovely girls.

DONALD: Say their names, sweetheart.

PATRICIA: Maria, Pinta and Nina.

DONALD: Thank you. Thank you. Did you say they were lovely?

PATRICIA: Yes, I did. Lovely and so polite and prolific.

DONALD: They gave me six grandchildren.

PATRICIA: [*Peeved.*] I know full well how many grandchildren they gave you! You don't have to remind me because I don't give a horse's ass how many grandchildren they gave you!

DONALD: [*Rises; warningly.*] Patricia, we can' t...

PATRICIA: Sorry, sorry. Sorry, sorry, sorry, sorry. It's not easy for a

PATRICIA: [*Cont'd.*] woman of my age to recognize she'll never be a...biological grandmother... with her own little grandchildren to put talcum on their tushies, to slip them into their little doggy pajamies, and to watch telly with them on Saturday night while eating french fries with ketchup! [*And she starts bawling.*]

DONALD: [*Embraces her.*] There, there, don't, honey. You'll be a grandmother one day. Jonathan...

PATRICIA: Jonathan is a bimbo! He still wears buttons on his fly!

DONALD: [*Laughing.*] That's what I've been trying to tell you. He...

PATRICIA: [*Suddenly flares.*] Are you laughing at my son? Is that what you're doing?

DONALD: Sorry, sorry. Sorry, sorry, sorry, sorry.

PATRICIA: And I'm sorry, sweetheart. Lately, I have great difficulty restraining myself. It seems the older I get the more I have to give vent to my emotions.

DONALD: I understand. I have the same problem.
   [*They sit down again.*]

PATRICIA: In an odd way, I feel so much less inhibited, less fearful of what other people will think since I'm a senior citizen.

DONALD: Amazing. It's the same for me. I'm not afraid of any human being living on this planet anymore!

PATRICIA: You're not. I know you're not. You're incredible.

DONALD: I used to be such a fraidy-cat, all through elementary school, high school, college, my twenties, my thirties, all those years. But now? Did you see how I walked up to those four hoodlums who were sitting on our stoop last Sunday?

PATRICIA: Fearless. You were positively fearless.

DONALD: "Hey! Hey! You! Yeah, it's you I'm talking to. The four of you! Get off that stoop this minute or face the consequences! [*A beat.*] Yeah, yeah, I'm the consequences!"

PATRICIA: My heart stopped beating. I couldn't believe what I was hearing.

DONALD: Did they get off the stoop as I ordered?

PATRICIA: Each and every one of them. I can't imagine what you were thinking.

DONALD: I'll tell you what. I was thinking the worst thing that could happen is that they kill me. [*A beat.*] And then I was thinking, if they killed me, the worst thing that could happen is that I'd be laying in my coffin a few months earlier than I expected.

PATRICIA: Thank God they didn't hurt you.

DONALD: [*With insouciance.*] Who cares? Who cares? We have to go sometime. That's the deal we made when we started collecting our social security checks. We have to go so there'll be checks for the people who don't have to go until after we go!

PATRICIA: I am the luckiest woman in the world to be married to you.

DONALD: I know. [*A beat.*] Now I have to say, in all honesty, I do like Jonathan. He has a wonderful sense of humor.

PATRICIA: Doesn't he? Isn't he amusing?

DONALD: I can't find the words to describe how amusing he is.

PATRICIA: Now it's my turn to be honest with you. Your first wife . . .

DONALD: Bertha.

PATRICIA: Yes. Bertha. You lived with her for over forty years and yet, after her demise, you were able to remarry another woman.

DONALD: You.

PATRICIA: Yes. Me. That you didn't loathe women after living with Bertha for over forty years . . . It's extraordinary.

DONALD: And a tribute to my first marriage to Bertha.

PATRICIA: Yes, that's what I wanted to say. But couldn't.

DONALD: I'm glad that you at last acknowledge... [*Turns.*] Did I hear the doorbell ring?

PATRICIA: I didn't...

DONALD: [*On his feet.*] I heard it. They're here! They're coming. Answer it, Pat. I'll open up a couple of bottles of mineral water. Who do you think it is? Who do you think is the first one?

PATRICIA: [*This is silly; not at all easy for her.*] I have no idea. Donald, do we have to go through with this? It's ...

DONALD: You promised! You gave me your solemn word: I don't want to hear anymore of that! Now will you or won't you answer the door? Our guests are arriving!

PATRICIA: [*Resolved to do her best; moves to door, taking off cap.*] Yes, yes, I'm going, I am. I'll see who it is. [*At door.*] Are you ready?

DONALD: [*Removes cap; brushes off uniform.*] Ready.

PATRICIA: The party begins. [*She throws open door.*]

DONALD: [*Hushed voice.*] Who? Who is it?

PATRICIA: [*Hasn't the faintest.*] It's... It's... It's...

DONALD: Who! Who!

PATRICIA: [*Desperately.*] Harry James!

[*DONALD gasps loudly; beyond his wildest dreams. PATRICIA beams. Thank God she came up with a winner.*]

PATRICIA: [*Cont'd.*] Come in, come in, Mr. James. We are so, so happy you were able to come to our party this afternoon.

[*Her eyes follow an imaginary HARRY JAMES as he enters; she closes the door.*]

May I introduce you to my husband, Mr. James? [*A beat.*] Harry? You prefer I call you Harry? [*A beat.*] Yes, of course. We are like old friends. My husband has been a fan of yours for... eons. He loves your music. [*Clears throat; formally.*] Harry, I have the distinct pleasure of introducing you to my husband, Mr. Donald Lumley, an amply decorated veteran of the 1941-1945 conflagration.

DONALD: Mr. James... Harry. [*Swallows.*] Harry, this is an event, the likes of which I have not experienced since I saw Frank Sinatra at the Paramount Theater on October 12th, 1944. [*Hand on heart.*] I'm choked. I'm literally choked up and can't stop my voice from trembling.

PATRICIA: Donald probably has the largest collection of your records in the Tri-state area.

DONALD: [*Emotionally.*] My favorites are "You Made Me Love You," "I Cried for You," "I Don't Want to Walk Without You," "I Had the Craziest Dream," "I've Heard That Song Before," and so many, many more, including your trumpet virtuosity with Benny Goodman in "Sing, Sing, Sing," and . . . I could go on and on . . . but it hurts too much, Harry, for me to remember those days of yesteryore.

PATRICIA: [*At record collection.*] These are all your recordings, Harry. They're on 78s and V discs that Donald collected in the service and here are tapes and CDs . . . [*She plays a record or CD. We hear James's "I Walk Alone," or another of his tunes.*]

    [*Holding out hand.*] Donald.

    [DONALD *puffs out his chest and takes her extended hand. They dance, lovers on a cloud. After a moment or two,* DONALD *stops the dance.*]

DONALD: We should return to our guest, sweetheart. Thank you for the dance. [*He kisses her on cheek; moves to* HARRY.] We dance to your music all the time, Harry. There's nothing around like it. Do sit down. Make yourself comfortable. My home is yours.

    [DONALD *sits on last folding chair, right;* HARRY *on the next;* PATRICIA *on the third.*]

PATRICIA: May I get you a drink, Harry? A bourbon? A scotch? A banana daiquiri?

DONALD: I didn't know you could make a banana daiquiri, dear.

PATRICIA: Oh, yes, I learned years ago. From a native of Patagonia.

DONALD: [*A thoughtful beat; whispers to* HARRY.] Don't take everything my wife says literally. She tends to exaggerate a bit. [*Then.*] Honey, why don't we wait until the others arrive before

DONALD: [*Cont'd.*] we serve drinks? I would like to start with champagne, to toast the occasion.

PATRICIA: Shall we wait for the others, Harry?

DONALD: [*Leans towards him.*] I'm sorry. I didn't hear you. What did you say? [*Bursts out in laughter; to* PATRICIA.] He said he already drank half a bottle of bourbon this morning. He prefers to wait.

PATRICIA: As you like, Harry. I don't know if you're aware of it, but besides celebrating VJ Day we're also celebrating our first anniversary.

DONALD: Does that surprise you, Harry?

PATRICIA: It surprised everyone. Our children were vehemently against our getting married.

DONALD: They thought we were too old to go a second time around.

PATRICIA: They were embarrassingly wrong. We've never been as happy as we've been this past year.

DONALD: You know the expression "made for each other?"

PATRICIA: We were unequivocally made for each other. And, mind you, we both had excellent first marriages.

DONALD: No doubt about it. Excellent first marriages.

PATRICIA: I was sincerely in love with my first husband.

DONALD: And I my first wife. She was a sweetheart, an absolute sweetheart.

PATRICIA: And yet...

DONALD: Patty and I...

PATRICIA: We were made for each other.

DONALD: Unequivocally.

PATRICIA: The fact is we do everything together.

DONALD: Everything. Golf, stretching exercises, a two mile walk in the park every morning...

PATRICIA: Trips to the museum, Atlantic City, an East Side restaurant at least once a week, the cinema... We love the cinema.

DONALD: And I'll tell you a secret, Harry, we have an incredibly active sex life.

[PATRICIA *grins widely, rolls her eyes upwards in gratitude.*]

PATRICIA: My husband is a regular hound dog. It's exhausting.

DONALD: Fortunately, we exercise and eat a lot of fish!

PATRICIA: What you don't know, Harry, is that we met on VJ Day, fifty years ago.

DONALD: In Manila. We were on active duty.

[*They nibble on finger foods, offering the same to* HARRY.]

PATRICIA: I was stationed aboard a hospital ship while Donald was temporarily stationed at Subic Bay, waiting reassignment.

DONALD: By pure happenstance, we were both on leave in Manila.

PATRICIA: I remember I was having drinks with some friends in an unspeakably dark and dirty bar called The Piggly Wiggly.

DONALD: I just walked into The Piggly Wiggly when someone ran in and shouted the war was over! The Japanese had surrendered!

PATRICIA: And everyone was shouting in the street, "The war is over! The war is over!"

DONALD: For a minute or two minutes or three minutes there was total silence, not a peep out of anybody.

PATRICIA: But then... [*Jumps to her feet.*] ...everybody in the bar started screaming and yelling...

DONALD: [*Jumps to his feet.*] It was absolute pandemonium!

PATRICIA: Chaos! It was sheer chaos!

DONALD: I don't know how it happened...

PATRICIA: But the next thing I know...

DONALD: We were holding hands!

PATRICIA: Jumping up and down!

DONALD: Yelling to beat the band!

PATRICIA: Singing, too!

PATRICIA/DONALD: [*Singing.*] "Happy days are here, are here again [*Or some such tune.*]

DONALD: We hit it off!

PATRICIA: Right from the start! From the very beginning!

DONALD: It was like we were drunk, drunk on the exhiliration of being together!

PATRICIA: We couldn't stop . . . touching one another.

DONALD: And we danced. For hours and hours. To the jukebox.

[*They dance, barely moving.*]

"I'll Be With You In Apple Blossom Time."

PATRICIA: "Be Careful It's My Heart."

DONALD: "There Will Never Be Another You."

PATRICIA: "People Will Say We're In Love."

[*Eyes only for each other; stop dancing; whisper.*]

DONALD: We hit it off.

PATRICIA: Unequivocally.

DONALD: What did we do? What did we talk about? How did the day go so fast?

PATRICIA: And the night. Where did it go?

DONALD: I remember I got back to the base late and the C.O. bawled me out, but I didn't hear anything or see anything. My head was filled with you.

PATRICIA: And mine with you, only you. [*Breaks out of it; moves to sit beside* HARRY.] You see, Harry, so much was going on during those weeks, there was such an incredible fever, excitement . . .

DONALD: [*Sits on his chair.*] Before we knew it, we were being shipped back to the States.

PATRICIA: We were going home, to live with our parents, to be with our friends.

DONALD: There were major decisions to be made.

PATRICIA: I didn't want to pursue a nursing career I couldn't, not after...

DONALD: She had nightmares. She still has them. Of the soldiers brought on the hospital ship ... to die there.

PATRICIA: I often wonder, do they know the direction the world has taken since ... then? Are they grieved by the turn of events? Do they think now that they died in vain, for no earthly purpose ... or reason? Do they know that we've forgotten all about them?

DONALD: That's not true, Patricia. Not everyone! Not some of us! [*Softer tone.*] Besides, this is not the time to go into it. We're here to memorialize the very men you're speaking of. [*To* HARRY.] I was always interested in the law so...

PATRICIA: Donald went to law school. I went to City College to become a guidance counselor at a junior high school in the Bronx.

DONALD: I eventually specialized in real estate law and did quite well for myself.

PATRICIA: As for Donald and me...

DONALD: We wrote to one another, regularly...

PATRICIA: We spoke on the phone, frequently...

DONALD: And we dated ... at the beginning...

PATRICIA: You see, Harry, the Bronx and Brooklyn are at opposite ends of the world.

DONALD: It took me over an hour, by subway, to get to her place from mine. And that's not counting the long walk to and from the subways.

PATRICIA: Even when we were going to school we had part-time jobs.

DONALD: I used to work six days and Sunday mornings, too. It wasn't that easy getting together. [*A beat.*] She started going out with other men.

PATRICIA: And?

DONALD: I started going out with other women. I was very sought-after as a young man.

PATRICIA: I didn't go out with other men. I went out with Herman, my first husband.

DONALD: The next thing I know she calls me and tells me she's getting married and moving to Chicago.

PATRICIA: Herman worked for Metropolitan Life. They offered him a substantial raise and promotion.

DONALD: I didn't waste any time. Within three months I was married myself, to Bertha Hoffmueller, a wonderful gregarious and attractive woman who worked as a buyer for S. Klein's on Union Square.

PATRICIA: Herman was six feet two inches tall, a very handsome and dynamic man. He loved to travel and we visited, during the course of our marriage, London, Paris, Rome, Budapest, Casablanca...

DONALD: [*Interrupts.*] Harry may I speak to you a moment, privately? [*To* PATRICIA.] Excuse us. [*He leads* HARRY *to the side, right, looks back to* PATRICIA, *thinks she might be able to overhear him, leads* HARRY *further downstage; whispers.*]
     You won't get the truth out of her when it comes to her late husband. Take my word for it, he was not a nice man. And he was taller than six foot two. Whenever he was in a room his head would be up there in the chandelier. He'd be talking to the lightbulbs. A very unsociable man. They used to come to New York from Chicago a couple of times a year, to go to the the ater, restaurants... Pat would phone and our families would get together for a few hours. It was painful. Bertha and Pat didn't get along, Herman and I had nothing in common, the kids didn't hit it off, and every time I saw Pat it'd break my heart. I... I still had very strong feelings about her and...We stopped seeing one another. That was the end of it until...Bertha passed away several years ago and I phoned Pat, out of the blue, out of loneliness, out of despair, without knowing that Herman had passed away ten years before Bertha did.

PATRICIA: Donald?

DONALD: Yes, dear?

PATRICIA: I feel abandoned.

DONALD: I'm sorry, sweetheart. Forgive me.
[*Moving to her,* HARRY *in tow.*] I was just telling Harry how we finally got back together again.

PATRICIA: You may think it's silly of me, Harry, but, in my opinion, what happened between Donald and me qualifies as divine intervention.

DONALD: [*Listening a beat.*] What was that?

PATRICIA: What was what?

DONALD: Didn't you hear the doorbell ring?

PATRICIA: I didn't hear anything.

DONALD: Did you hear it, Harry? [*Tilts head towards him.*] Harry heard it, too. You should see a doctor about your hearing, dear.

PATRICIA: Do you want me to . . . ?

DONALD: [*Moving to door.*] No, I'll. get it. You entertain Harry. [*Throws open door; gasps.*]

PATRICIA: Who? Who is it?

DONALD: [*Turns to her in awe.*] What does the name Betty Grable mean to you?

PATRICIA: Noooo.

DONALD: [*Nodding fervently.*] Yes! Yes! [*Turns to door.*] Miss Grable, won't you . . . ?

PATRICIA: Wait! Wait! [*Waves for him to join her.*]

DONALD: [*To imaginary* BETTY.] Excuse me, Miss Grable. A moment. I'll be right back. [*Rushes to* PATRICIA; *whispers impatiently.*] What? What is it?

PATRICIA: [*Whispers.*] They're divorced!

DONALD: Who's divorced?

PATRICIA: Harry James and Betty Grable:

DONALD: [*Horrified.*] What a *faux pas* we made inviting her!

PATRICIA: We didn't invite her! You invited her!

DONALD: She was at the door! I didn't...What should we do?

PATRICIA: Put her in the ping-pong room!

DONALD: The ping-pong room?

PATRICIA: We'll keep them apart. They'll never meet. We'll avoid a major social embarrassment!

DONALD: Good idea. Excellent idea. Leave it to me. [*He rushes back to door; expansively.*] Come in, Miss Grable. Do come in. Let me introduce you to my lovely wife, Patricia.

PATRICIA: I am delighted, overwhelmingly delighted to meet you, Miss Grable — I loved your acting in "Down Argentine Way" and "I Wake Up Screaming." You were superb. Now if you'll follow me...[*Leads* BETTY *to the ping-pong room.*] You'll have privacy in here and you won't be annoyed by any of the other guests. We'll drop in now and then to converse with you. Help yourself to anything in the refrigerator. [*She closes door.*] She'll be happy. It must be so annoying for a star to...[*Listening a beat.*] Ah, the doorbell! I'll get it, dear. [*She moves to door which has remained open; sees guests; turns to* DONALD; *glowing.*] You are going to be very pleased with those who have taken the time off from their pressing duties to be with us here today. [*Turns to door; announces.*]
   General Douglas MacArthur!
   [*She salutes.* DONALD *snaps stiffly to attention, clicks his heels and salutes smartly.*]

PATRICIA: [*Cont'd.*] General Dwight D. Eisenhower! Admiral Chester Nimitz! [*She salutes, twice.* DONALD *salutes and clicks his heels together, twice.*]

DONALD: Sirs, this is indeed a great, great honor, one that I thought would never occur during my lifetime. [*Gestures.*] Please, take a seat next to Harry James, the world-renowned trumpet player. If any of you would like to converse with Betty Grable, the pin-up girl to millions of servicemen, she's in the ping-pong room. [*Turns.*] Patty...

PATRICIA: [*Now enjoying it all.*] One second, dear. There are more guests coming. I see...[*Hand to heart.*] I don't believe it!

DONALD: Who? Who's coming?

PATRICIA: [*To entering guest.*] I am so thrilled by your presence at our party, Mrs. Roosevelt. I can't describe... [*Listening a beat.*] Of course. Eleanor. [*A proud look to* DONALD.] Eleanor, I must tell you, both my husband and I worshipped your late husband. It was a terrible shock to us when we learned the reason why we never saw him standing up. But do come in and make yourself comfortable.

DONALD: Having you in my home is beyond my wildest dreams... Eleanor. [*Listening a beat.*] Donald. Radioman 3rd Class Donald Lumley. Incidentally, I visited your home in Hyde Park last summer. Lovely place. Excellent landscaping. And the antique oriental rug in your living-room... It must have cost you a bloody fortune! [*Moving towards the empty chairs with her.*]
　　We have some guests here I'm sure you know. Some military men who served under your husband. [*He improvises introductions, sotto voce; chats, laughs, offers food, etc.*]

PATRICIA: [*To entering guests.*] I'm speechless! I don't know what to say to you, Mr. Einstein. Thank you. Thank you so very much for taking the time from your scientific work to be with us today. [*Gestures.*] My husband, who is chatting over there with Mrs. Roosevelt and Admiral Nimitz will introduce you to our guests. [*Turns back to doorway.*]
　　Is that... Is that really you, Joe Louis? Ahh, how kind... But who's that with you? Lou Gehrig, the Yankee slugger? Come in, come in, gentlemen, please. My first husband talked about you two incessantly. [*Gestures.*] Do introduce yourselves to my second husband, Donald. Oh, yes, I was married twice. It does have its advantages.
　　[*Laughs frivolously; turns to doorway; in amazement.*] Noooo... It's not true. You came... You... You travelled three thousand miles to be here with me on this... on this the most important day of my life.

DONALD: [*Moving to her.*] Patricia...

PATRICIA: [*Ignores him.*] How can I ever repay you, Mr. Gable, except...

DONALD: Patricia...

PATRICIA: [*Parodies Judy Garland.*] ... to let you know ... that my heart is beating like a hammer ... whenever I see you in a picture show ...

DONALD: Patricia, I'm talking to you!

PATRICIA: Excuse me, Mr. Gable.
[*Shouts at* DONALD.] What is it? I am talking to Clark Gable!

DONALD: [*Through clenched teeth.*] We have other guests, Patricia! They are hungry. They are thirsty. I cannot do everything myself. I am, whether you and Clark Gable want to recognize it or not ... [*Shouts.*] ... a senior citizen!

PATRICIA: [*Heartfelt.*] And I am such a fool!

DONALD: No, no, you're not! I am! I am!

PATRICIA: You're everything to me.

DONALD: I would long ago have been a bag of bones if not for you.

PATRICIA: I love you, Donny-o.

DONALD: And I, you, Patty m'girl.

PATRICIA: [*Brightly.*] I'll introduce Mr. Gable to our guests and pass the canapés and hors d 'oeuvres. Mr. Gable ... if you'll follow me ... [*She moves towards empty chairs; improvises introductions, sotto voce; chats, laughs, offers food, etc.*]

DONALD: Ah, the doorbell! I have it, sweetheart! [*Moves to doorway; looks out.*] Why, it's ... Rita Hayworth! [*Turns.*] Rita Hayworth is here, Pat! She looks absolutely stunning.

PATRICIA: What is she wearing?

DONALD: A white, satin nightgown and a black, lacy brassiere! [*Turns to Rita.*] Come in, come in, Rita. No, no, you're not late. Who's that with you? Ava Gardner? Come in, yes, you, don't be shy. You brought ... Lana Turner? Wonderful! And do I see Eva Marie Saint and Rhonda Fleming out there? Who else? Dinah Shore and Dina Merrill? With Dana Andrews? Wonderful! Wonderful! Do come in, all of you! [*Laughing.*]

DONALD: [*Cont'd.*] Oh, this is wonderful, terrific, the cream on the cake! [*He closes door; crosses with his guests.*] Pat, I want to introduce you to Rita, Ava, Lana, Eva, Rhonda, Dinah, Dina and Dana.

PATRICIA: I'm delighted to meet each and every one of you. And may I introduce you to Harry, Douglas, Dwight, Chester, Eleanor, Albert, Joe, Lou and Clark.

DONALD: [*Opens bottle of champagne.*] And if any of you would like to.speak to Betty Grable, she's in the ping-pong room. [*The cork pops out of the bottle.*]

PATRICIA: [*Applauding.*] Bravo! Bravo! Don't spill any, dear.
     [DONALD *pours only a drop in several glasses on table— for the guests; he fills two glasses for* PATRICIA *and himself.*]

PATRICIA: [*Cont'd.*] Everyone, everyone, may I have your attention, please? [*A beat.*] First of all, let me say, my husband and I can't thank you enough for coming today.

DONALD: Speaking for myself, I am genuinely appreciative of your taking the time off from your incredibly busy schedules to be at our party.

PATRICIA: [*Taking champagne from* DONALD.] Please, help yourselves to the champagne. I'd like to make a toast.

DONALD: [*Applauding.*] Speech! Speech!

PATRICIA: [*To guests.*] My dear ... heroes, for that is what you are to me ... my heroes. Many of you sacrificed yourselves, unequivocally, to help bring about peace in the world ... whatever peace we have in the world. Like the peace we had in Korea, and the peace we had in Vietnam, and the peace we had in Belfast and in Jerusalem and in Afghanistan and in Bosnia and so on and so forth ... as we listened over the years to the well-tailored politicians intoning "this is the war to end all wars, for a better world of love and brotherhood, never again will we slaughter the innocent children for the sake of flag or boundary, for the sake of religious, ethnic, cultural differences, or for this, that and the other thing, never again until we go to war ... the next time.

DONALD: [*Peeved.*] Patricia, you are being rude to our guests! They came here to join us in a celebration of victory, not to listen to a diatribe of your dissatisfaction with politicians!

PATRICIA: [*Firmly.*] I'll be done in a minute. Please, be patient.

[*To guests.*] I often wonder, do they, those who died fifty years ago, do they know the direction the world has taken since then? Are they grieved by the turn of events? Do they think now that they died in vain, for no earthly purpose or reason? Do they know that we've forgotten all about them?

DONALD: [*Almost a whisper.*] Patricia, I asked you . . .

PATRICIA: [*Won't be silent.*] I often wonder, if they came to my bedside in the middle of the night, and they stood around me with their white, bloodless faces staring down at me, and one of them said, "What should we have done, Patty? Did we do wrong? Did we act stupidly, precipitously? Should we have taken another direction with our lives?" [*Turns from one imaginary guest to another.*] I know what I would say to him. I would say . . . [*Finger to lips.*] "Shhh. It's over. It doesn't matter anymore. But for the sake of conversation . . . You should have done as the others did. As we did. Those of us who survived. Hang back. Drag your feet. Don't look directly at them. Look behind you. Look to the side of you. Look down at your shoes. But not at them, in their uniforms and ribbons, in their well-tailored clothes. Fight them. Fight them so as not to fight. Complain of illness, backache, flatfoot, perversity, maladjustment, dependency, principle, whatever comes to mind, whatever the cost in face or status. Do not go. Wave a flag. Cry Jesus, Hare Krishna, Holy Moses. Cross the border. Fly to Patagonia. Do not go. It will all be forgotten. Amends will be made. Brotherhood affirmed. Economic benefits derived. Do not go. It will all be forgotten. As you have been forgotten." [*Turns to stare at DONALD.*]

DONALD: This is not what we planned. This is not what we said we'd do. I demand, as a matter of courtesy, equal time! [*He turns at once to guests.*] My esteemed and honored guests. Permit me to go on record as saying that I am categorically in disagreement with Patricia. [*Turns to her.*] My second wife. [*Back to guests.*] The indisputable truth is that we won the war. We were

DONALD: [*Cont'd.*] victorious. We triumphed over the forces of despotism and tyranny. Patricia dismisses or chooses to ignore what was at stake when we went to war. If we as a nation had not responded with military might, if we as Americans had not put our lives on the line, everything we valued would have been taken away from us. Everything! We fought so that we could live as a free people. Imagine what it would have been like if we lost the war! If this country of ours was occupied by the forces of despotism and tyranny! Is there any doubt in anyone's mind that we would have been totally dominated and enslaved by a foreign government? We had no choice but to do what we did. Fight. Defend ourselves. Participate in a world struggle for decency and dignity! Who died and who lived was in the hands of the Almighty. It is . . . the essence of humankind to protect the young, the infirm, the helpless, to sacrifice life if need be for an ideal that goes beyond survival. Therein lies our glory and our redemption. Without it we are nothing. We are less than nothing. We are shadows on the wall of a cave. [*A beat.*] My esteemed and honored guests, we won the war. We were victorious. That unparalleled achievement is ingrained in our national consciousness and will never be forgotten, but it will always be a source to us for strength, for pride, and for eternal gratitude to those who made the ultimate sacrifice.

PATRICIA: Donald? [*He turns to her.*] What does that mean, we won the war?

DONALD: [*More in desperation than conviction.*] We won: We were victorious! We triumphed: We raised the flag on Iwo Jima! We bombed the oppressors to smithereens! We brought the fascists and the imperialists down to their knees and stuck their snouts into the muck of their own rotting corpses! No small achievement, my dear! Nothing to be maligned or demeaned or casually dismissed!

PATRICIA: But what does it add up to? What have we won? What has changed? Where are we today, fifty years later? Are we really victorious?

DONALD: [*Losing it.*] I'm not going to quarrel with you, Patricia! That's enough! It's enough! I don't want to hear another

DONALD: [*Cont'd.*] word...! [*He breathes heavily, staring at her, an anguished expression.*] I am sorry. I am so sorry.

PATRICIA: [*Anguished as well.*] Oh, why? why? why?

DONALD: I love you.

PATRICIA: I love you.

DONALD: My biggest fear is to lose you.

PATRICIA: I won't let it happen. I swear. I promise.
    [*They are a distance apart; they do not move towards each other.*]

DONALD: Happy anniversary, my dear, sweet, lovely wife.

PATRICIA: I bless the day I met you.

DONALD: Do we begin our party now?

PATRICIA: Yes, yes, we mustn't be rude to our guests! [*Turns.*] Happy, happy anniversary, everyone! Please, eat, drink, ask if you want anything, need anything... [*Fills two glasses with champagne.*] This is a day of celebration! [*Looks about.*] Where's Harry? Did Harry leave? [*Listens a beat.*] He's in the ping-pong room? With Betty Grable? Ahh, that is wonderful. I knew there'd be a reconciliation. I knew it all along.
    [DONALD *has put on the cassette player. We now hear Benny Goodman's "Sing, Sing, Sing," or some similar tune.*]

DONALD: [*Approaching* PATRICIA.] Mrs. Lumley?

PATRICIA: Yes, Mr. Lumley?

DONALD: May I have this dance?

PATRICIA: This one and the next one and the one after that, too.
    [*And they start dancing the Lindy, as it was done at the Palladium fifty years ago.*
    Lights congeal on them dancing in the empty room.
    A shaft of light isolates them in a sea of darkness.
    Lights and music fade out.]

Lanford Wilson

YOUR EVERYDAY GHOST STORY

Your Everyday Ghost Story by Lanford Wilson. Copyright © 1996 by Lanford Wilson. All rights reserved. Reprinted by permission of International Creative Management.

CAUTION: Professionals and amateurs are hereby warned that *Your Everyday Ghost Story* by Lanford Wilson is subject to a royalty. It is fully protected under the copyright laws of the United States of America, and of all countries covered by the International Copyright Union (including the Dominion of Canada and the rest of the British Commonwealth), and of all countries covered by the Pan-American Convention and the Universal Copyright Convention, and of all countries with which the United States has reciprocal copyright relations. All rights, including professional, amateur, motion picture, recitation, lecturing, public reading, radio broadcasting, television, video or sound taping, all other forms of mechanical or electronic reproduction, such as information storage and retrieval systems and photocopying, and the rights of translation into foreign languages, are strictly reserved. Particular emphasis is placed upon the question of readings, permission for which must be secured from the author's agent in writing.

Your Everyday Ghost Story was originally commissioned by Alma Delfina Group, San Francisco (THE AIDS PROJECT — PIECES OF THE QUILT). The play can only be performed with the permission of this group, c/o Mame Hunt, Magic Theatre, Building D, Fort Mason Center, San Francisco, CA 94123.

For all other rights of any kind contact the Author's agent: Bridget Aschenberg, International Creative Management, Inc., 40 West 57th Street, New York, NY 10019.

Lanford Wilson

Lanford Wilson received the 1980 Pulitzer Prize for Drama and the New York Drama Critics Circle Award for *Talley's Folly*. He is a founding member of the Circle Repertory Company in New York and was a resident playwright for the company from 1969 to 1995.

His work at Circle Rep includes: *The Family Continues* (1972), *The HOT L Baltimore* (1973), *The Moundbuilders* (1975), *Serenading Louie* (1976), *5th of July* (1978), *Talley's Folly* (1980), *A Tale Told* (1981), *Angels Fall* (1982), *Burn This* (1987), and *Redwood Curtain* (1992), all directed by Marshall Mason.

His other plays include *The Gingham Dog* (1966), *The Rimers of Eldritch* (1967), *Lemon Sky* (1969), and some twenty produced one-acts, such as *Brontosaurus* (1977) and *Thymus Vulgaris* (1982). He has also written the libretto for Lee Hoiby's opera of Tennessee Williams' *Summer and Smoke*, and two television plays, *Taxi!* and *The Migrants* (based on a short story by Tennessee Williams).

Other awards include the New York Critics' Award, the Outer Critics Circle Award and an Obie for *The HOT L Baltimore*, an Obie for *The Mound Builders*, a Drama-Logue Award for *5th of July* and *Talley's Folly*, the Vernon Rice award for *The Rimers of Eldritch*, and Tony Award nominations for *Talley's Folly*, *5th of July*, and *Angels Fall*. He is the recipient of the Brandeis University Creative Arts Award in Theatre Arts and the Institute of Arts and Letters Award.

He makes his home in Sag Harbor, New York.

CHARACTERS

KEVIN

LANCE

Just a bench, wrought iron and wood, but I don't see this as a bench play. I think they stand or lean and walk around most of the time, except at the beginning and end.

KEVIN *and* LANCE *are reasonably attractive young men in their early 30's. Kevin talks a lot; that's partly just him and partly anxiety. Lance is uneasy at times but not unsympathetic.*

The scene is bathed in an exaggerated golden sunset of a late autumn afternoon. Dark shadows upstage.

LANCE *is sitting on the bench, looking out. He is either unconcerned about his dress or thinks a writer should dress shabbily.*

KEVIN (*Offstage.*): [*Calling.*] Lance!

[*Lance didn't want to see this guy but he covers it well. He stands as Kevin enters. Kevin dresses smartly.*]

LANCE: Oh. Hi, Kevin — God, you look great!

KEVIN: Are you kidding, I've got cancer!

LANCE: [*Taken aback, recovering.*] No! Kevin! [*Very awkward.*] That's terrible. Are you sure?

KEVIN: You knew or you wouldn't have said I looked great.

LANCE: No, you do look great. You look great.

KEVIN: Yeah, but you expected me to look like shit.

LANCE: Somebody told me.

KEVIN: So I suppose they also told you I have AIDS.

LANCE: [*Fakes surprise.*] Oh, no. That's — [*Gives up.*] No, yeah, I heard. I think it sucks. They said you were in the hospital, I'm glad you're out.

KEVIN: [*Ironically.*] And you were only pretending you didn't know so you wouldn't embarrass me, or remind me. That's kind.

LANCE: I thought maybe you didn't want people to know.

KEVIN: Everybody and his fucking cat knows. It makes it real interesting walking down the street.

LANCE: What are they doing for you?

KEVIN: They're fucking killing me. I've got chemo and radiation four times a week. They're taking things out of my lungs and my ass, my liver. I've had biopsies on glands I haven't used in years.

LANCE: Oh, God.

KEVIN: They've got radiation machines big as a house, well, I don't know, I close my eyes. They can't *find* any more veins, I don't *have* any more veins. My legs, my arms, are black and blue all over, I'm doing a reverse Michael Jackson, it's horrifying.

LANCE: What's making your arms black and — ?

[KEVIN *makes a shoving motion into the veins of his arm.*]

KEVIN: Bruises. From the chemo.

LANCE: Oh, Christ, it's intravenous?

KEVIN: You didn't know that? And you call yourself a writer. You're getting very pale, you aren't going to faint, are you?

LANCE: No, I'm fine, but —

KEVIN: [*He can be a little malicious.*] Yeah, I'm learning a lot of shit no one should have to know. On top of everything else they made me stop smoking. Well, I was coughing up my guts. Which I used to think was only an expression. I'm sorry, I hope you haven't just eaten or anything.

LANCE: No, I —

KEVIN: Also it makes you stink.

LANCE: What does?

KEVIN: The chemo. Nobody tells you that part. It makes you smell like . . . Death.

LANCE: Oh.

KEVIN: Well, I'm sorry, but that's what it smells like. [*Beat.*] They fired me. From that fucking display studio. They said I was

KEVIN: [*Cont'd.*] becoming irrational. Who would be rational. Of course I'm becoming irrational! Assholes!

LANCE: They can't fire you, it's illegal.

KEVIN: It's *Philadelphia* all over again. Write a movie. Make a fortune. Call it Patchogue, New York. [*Note: pronounced PATCH-hog.*]

LANCE: It doesn't scan.

KEVIN: I know, but that's where the bastards' studio is.

LANCE: I can't write movies, the proper misogynistic tone keeps eluding me.

KEVIN: And you don't write unfunny gay characters.

LANCE: That was *Philadelphia*, it's been done.

[*Lance is trying to wind up the conversation.*]

KEVIN: I know, you've got to go finish the last chapter of the Great American Novel. Look at you. Trying to make your escape. You always do that. You did it to me.

LANCE: No, really. I'll call you —

KEVIN: You will not. Everyone knows you run from hospitals and sick people like the plague. Well, in this case it is the plague so you have every right.

LANCE: I'm sorry, I just —

KEVIN: "Sorry" doesn't cut it. God save us from your fucking artistic temperament. All the novels and stories and TV shit, none of your gay characters have a care in the world.

LANCE: They have cares, Kevin. Only I do write people who are toilet trained. They're not pawing around in their own feces.

KEVIN: Oh, that's attractive. I happen to think pawing around in feces is where good writing comes from. That's just a lay opinion, you understand.

LANCE: If you want stories about how mom and pop and the boy next door hated us, read someone else.

KEVIN: The boy next door did not hate me. [*Beat.*] Do you avoid

KEVIN: [*Cont'd.*] just *everything* that's a little messy? Messy is what life is largely about. There are enough writers avoiding messy, we don't need you doing it.

LANCE: What is this? Nobody needs another one of your every-damn-day ghost stories either.

KEVIN: You are the weirdest combination of self-destruction and denial. You just don't want to go there, do you? Is it the monstrosity, the face-to-face with it, the loss? —

LANCE: — I have a very tenuous grip on reality, here, Kevin —

KEVIN: —Does all this rotting death just remind you of your own? That's the same for everyone, honey. "It is Margaret you mourn for" and don't forget it.

LANCE: Come on, you look weak but you're very strong. I look strong and everything scares the shit out of me.

KEVIN: Well, it damn well should; with the way you drink it won't be pleasant. I mean you're healthy now, but: liver transplants, kidney failure, bypasses. Isn't there a history of emphysema in your family? Can you smell it? Smell my hands.

LANCE: — Come on. It's the whole fucking set-up —

KEVIN: — Even in your work, you dodge and glance, finesse, waft your point across the night air —

LANCE: — I've been told —

KEVIN: — Feint, parry. What are you afraid of? Going down there and getting lost? Drowning, feeling, losing it?

LANCE: *People should not die!*

KEVIN: Oh. Well. I don't know. *Some* people shouldn't die, other people probably should but they never do. *One* should not die. One's friends shouldn't die. One's assistant shouldn't die. I heard about Fred. I'm sorry.

LANCE: I know. I still can't believe it.

KEVIN: Who's going to edit all your stuff?

LANCE: I don't know. I can't think about it. Someone at the publishing house. I can't think about it.

KEVIN: How was he?

LANCE: I was going to see him, a couple of us called the hospital —

KEVIN: — He worshipped you for Christsake —

LANCE: — We were going to go! They said he was scheduled for another operation —

KEVIN: I don't believe you. Jesus!

LANCE: — so we didn't go that day.

KEVIN: And he died. They do that. Poor you. He'd been in and out of the hospital five months; you had plenty of opportunity.

LANCE: I know. Fuck you. Fred was weird; he never told anyone. You don't know what people want.

KEVIN: Acknowledgment! Friendship! Jesus! What good is all your famous compassion if you deny everyone's pain?

LANCE: I feel bad enough without your —

KEVIN: [Overlapping completely.] — Please, please, please, you have to live with it, I don't have to live with it. Can you smell it?

LANCE: Come on. Yes. I don't even know you that well..

KEVIN: Isn't that always the way? And I thought we were close. I always tell people I know you.

LANCE: And it's just as well that they fired you; you didn't belong at that display house anyway.

KEVIN: It's called a job, darling.

LANCE: You're an interior designer, not a window display — person.

KEVIN: Sure. Christ, if they don't find a cure for this there won't be a window display left in America.

LANCE: I liked your shop.

KEVIN: Oh please. Never did two faggots crash and burn so spectacularly as Peter and I did with that shop. Forget the shop. The world can turn without another pouffe.

LANCE: I thought it was wonderful. The places you'd seen.

KEVIN: Tell it to the buying public. Nobody was interested in

KEVIN: [*Cont'd*] "exotic" that year, and you only get one crack; it's like fashion. Ten thousand yards of gorgeous, for want of a better word, "ethnic" fabric, all I got from it was a spectacular Halloween gown.

LANCE: Very spectacular.

KEVIN: What was important was learning so much about the people, the artisans, all over the world; that was important. Finding a really deep artistic integrity and originality in some 90 year old Chilean woman; their appreciation and pride.

That was rare: Two faggots with a great eye drifting through Malaysia, India, South America, Africa.

[*Not dreamy.*] Poling down mud rivers, passing grass huts, we get to a village of about 200, you've never seen silks like that, the colors alone — fuck it, nobody wanted it. Major miscalculation. Everything went *chintz* that year. Our whole shop looked like a sixties holdover. What a disaster. We sold three pillows and one chair that the bitch wanted re-upholstered. Four years in the planning, almost two years traveling, and the shop was only open two months; we didn't even make it through the summer. Three years later the guy who bought it for *11 cents on the dollar!* made a fucking killing. No lie, over a million and a half. You can't think about it.

LANCE: But the people, that was important.

KEVIN: And the memory of all that will go with us. Poof! It never happened. "Quick, grab the ruby slippers."

LANCE: I think it'd made a terrific movie. The two of you eating with the nomads and villagers, screaming over some puce cotton.

KEVIN: You can't use it unless it comes out funny.

LANCE: Kevin. Think about it. It's funny.

KEVIN: But with great depth and sensitivity.

LANCE: Poignant and funny. That's my trademark. Sort of a gay Around the World. Go everywhere from Mauritania to Timbuktu.

KEVIN: You're sweet and condescending as shit, but you're stupid.

KEVIN: [*Cont'd*] Why don't Americans know geography? And you call yourself a writer.

LANCE: Not lately. What?

KEVIN: Mauritania and Timbuktu, honey, are about 50 miles apart. Timbuktu is in Mali.

LANCE: Mali is in Africa? I thought it was in Asia.

KEVIN: Northwest Africa. *Way* up the Niger river. And we didn't go there; nobody goes there; there's nothing there. It's only famous because it must have rhymed with something.

LANCE: Call it *Kevin and Peter*.

KEVIN: Hmmm. Peter's been a brick, of course, Peter's been a saint. Peter's been a brick saint. A brick saint barber. "Stylist", he prefers.

LANCE: Peter is a saint.

KEVIN: Try being married to a saint. I've been giving him hell. I'm not being cool with this at all.

LANCE: I could tell. I had a trim yesterday, he must have known I knew; he didn't say a word. Well, neither did I. Peter's always so positive.

KEVIN: Yes, well, darling, now he really is. If you catch my drift.

LANCE: He always has been — Oh, God, no. Not him too.

KEVIN: He has a constitution of iron. I'm hoping he'll hold on till they find that mythological cure. In Valhalla. That great hall where all those who died in battle go. Thank God it turns out he's a fabulous hair-cutter. *Stars*, darling. Movie, TV, rock stars! Flocking to our little garage salon. Mercedes, Range Rovers and Jaguars lining the driveway. Who knew. Well, he's gorgeous and, as it turns out, majorly talented. We don't know how much longer he'll be able to work. He hasn't been sick at all, but who knows what will happen if word gets out... Still, we hope. But time is not our friend.

LANCE: Time is nobody's friend.

KEVIN: Tell me about it.

[*A reverie for a moment. No change other than that. Except:*]

LANCE: The memorial was beautiful. I mean, trust Peter. It was one of the only really spiritual experiences I've had at that sort of thing. It was out of town on this farm.

KEVIN: A farm?

LANCE: Well, a country place. There must have been over a hundred people. A big white house and a beautiful garden and then this meadow with a huge pond with trees around it.

KEVIN: That's Jim and Judy's place. It's beautiful out there.

LANCE: They had the memorial service in the garden. You know, the usual stories. Peter talked about living with you and all your travels and asked other people if they had anything to say. That was a little weird — we all just stood there, I guess everyone with his own thoughts. Then the girl whose place it was, Judy, started talking, and then one by one everyone began telling stories. It wasn't heavy, it was kind of light. Well, you're light.

KEVIN: [*Seeing it.*] In Kentucky we used to call that testifying. [*Beat. Then wary.*] What kind of "stories"?

LANCE: Anecdotes. Stories. Amusing things. You know.

KEVIN: Ummm.

LANCE: Then we all went through the gate and Peter had had them set up this huge —

KEVIN: — Excuse me, like what kind of "amusing things?"

LANCE: I can't remember exactly what anyone said, it was just —

KEVIN: You have a memory like a rat cage. I've heard you tell the complete scenario scene by scene of movies you saw when you were ten. What kind of amusing stories?

LANCE: Oh . . . Well, a lot of people just read postcards you had sent them from all over the world. [*Beat.*] OK. I said my most vivid memory was seeing you and Peter out at The Millstone one Halloween, you were both in total high drag —

KEVIN: That was my spectacular gown. And the one and only time I've gone out in drag.

LANCE: — And my date ditched me, so I caught a ride with you and Peter in your pickup. And you'd never driven in heels before but you refused to take them off because you said it was vulgar.

KEVIN: I remember it vividly. I did refuse and it is vulgar. [*Beat.*] And you all "went through this gate . . . ?"

LANCE: When we left the garden we went through the gate into the meadow overlooking the pond and they had set up this gigantic tent with a catered dinner. I had no idea. I think we all thought the last thing in the world we could do was eat, then we all discovered we were starving. Every seat had one of your silk pillows on it — incredible colors, a little piece of paper pinned to it with where it came from — that we took home as a kind of party favor.

KEVIN: Morbid. Thank God he found a use for those. They've been in storage for years.

LANCE: So we had a fabulous dinner as the sun set, with a string quartet yet, and after dinner we all took a glass of champagne and walked out around the pond, completely circled the pond, the damn thing is more like a lake. And Peter said, "To Kevin!" And we all yelled across the lake, "To Kevin!" and drank a toast to you.

KEVIN: And threw your glasses in the water.

LANCE: We did not. They were rented.

KEVIN: What ever happened to the grand gesture.

LANCE: Then we went back to the tent, about twenty of us, and got totally smashed. I couldn't get out of bed the next day. I have no memory of how I got home.

KEVIN: The kid knows how to throw a party. I told him I didn't want a memorial, just have a bunch of people over for dinner.

LANCE: He did. It was very moving, I still don't know why. I didn't describe it well, it was better than that.

KEVIN: You did OK. I mean, not for a writer, but I can imagine.

KEVIN: [*Cont'd.*] And God knows I know Peter's style. Aren't we all just crawling with style. Not you, of course. I bet you think there's something honest about dirty jeans. You can bet he planned every moment. You want to be sure, in your life, that they get one thing right.

LANCE: They got it right.

[*Kevin gets up from the bench. In a moment he'll walk away.*]

KEVIN: Well...

LANCE: It doesn't work, you know. It just makes it worse.

KEVIN: How's that?

LANCE: The memorials and tributes and — If it's designed to let you go. To help us get on with our lives, or accept the loss. It doesn't work.

KEVIN: Oh. No. That isn't want we want, I don't think. I think we're more selfish than that. [*Calling back.*] I think we want very badly for you to remember. [*Beat.*] I'll be back.

[*Kevin has walked into the dark shadows and is gone. Lance sits on the bench, as at the top, looking out, lost in thought. The lights fade to black.*]

THE END

Doug Wright

WILDWOOD PARK

Wildwood Park by Doug Wright. Copyright © 1997 by Doug Wright. All rights reserved. Reprinted by permission of International Creative Management, Inc.

Wildwood Park was originally commissioned and produced by McCarter Theatre, Princeton, N.J

CAUTION: Professionals and amateurs are hereby warned that *Wildwood Park* by Doug Wright is subject to a royalty. It is fully protected under the copyright laws of the United States of America, and of all countries covered by the International Copyright Union (including the Dominion of Canada and the rest of the British Commonwealth), and of all countries covered by the Pan-American Convention and the Universal Copyright Convention, and of all countries with which the United States has reciprocal copyright relations. All rights, including professional, amateur, motion picture, recitation, lecturing, public reading, radio broadcasting, television, video or sound taping, all other forms of mechanical or electronic reproduction, such as information storage and retrieval systems and photocopying, and the rights of translation into foreign languages, are strictly reserved. Particular emphasis is placed upon the question of readings, permission for which must be secured from the author's agent in writing.

All inquiries concerning rights should be addressed to the author's agent: International Creative Mangement, Inc., 40 West 57th Street, New York NY 10019, Attention: Sarah Jane Leigh.

Doug Wright

Doug Wright's other works include *The Stonewater Rapture*, *Interrogating the Nude*, *Dinosaurs*, *Lot 13: The Bone Violin*, *Wathanaland*, and a musical, *Buzzsaw Berkeley*, with songs by Michael John LaChiusa. His play *QUILLS*, based on the life and writing of the Marquis de Sade, received the 1995 Kesselring Prize for Best New American Play from the National Arts Club, and a Village Voice Obie Award for Outstanding Achievement in Playwriting. His work has been performed at New York Theater Workshop, the WPA Theater, the Yale Repertory Theater, Lincoln Center, the Wooly Mammoth Theater in Washington D.C., the McCarter Theater in New Jersey, the Cleveland Public Theater, the Geffen Theater in Los Angeles. He has been published by Dramatists Play Service, Heinemann Books' *New American Plays* anthology, *The Paris Review*, and now three times in the Applause Theatre Books' *Best American Short Plays* series. Wright's Television scripts include pilot projects for producer Norman Lear, and his film credits include screenplays for Fine Line Features, Fox Searchlight, Talking Wall Prictures, and Dreamworks SKG. He was named a McKnight Fellow for 1995-6 by the Playwrights Center in Minneapolis, and is a past recipient of the William L. Bradley Fellowship at Yale University, the Charles MacArthur Fellowship at the Eugene O'Neill Theater Center, an HBO Fellowship in playwriting, and the Alfred Hodder Fellowship at Princeton University.

CHARACTERS

MS. HAVILAND A realtor. She is middle-aged, a working mother. She wears an attractive quilted jacket, a navy skirt, and cloissonné jewelry. Her shoes are sensible, for walking.

DR. SIMIAN A prospective buyer. He is of indeterminate age, and wears an expensive suit. He is disarmingly handsome.

TIME: *Now.*

SETTING: *The stage is bare. The architecture, the furnishings and the props of the play are all invisible, and indicated by the actors through gesture—not in an overly-demonstrative or "mime" fashion, but simply and clearly, with minimal movement. Even when specific mention is made in the text of night stands, vanities, or fireplaces, these things are not seen; they are created through inference and the power of suggestion.*

A stark, sunny day. Both MS. HAVILAND *and* DR. SIMIAN *wear dark glasses, to shield their eyes from the offending light. They stand side-by-side, in front of the "house", gazing up at its exterior.*

DR. SIMIAN: The neighborhood. It exceeds my expectations. The trees are symmetrical. The mail-boxes have tiny flags. Along the alley, the trash cans all have matching lids.

MS. HAVILAND: It's well-tended.

DR. SIMIAN: It's almost perfection, isn't it?

[DR. SIMIAN *smiles at* MS. HAVILAND. *She does not return the gesture. There is a stiff pause.*]

MS. HAVILAND: How did you hear about this listing?

DR. SIMIAN: The newspaper.

MS. HAVILAND: The Real Estate section?

DR. SIMIAN: Yes.

MS. HAVILAND: That's not possible. Boulevard Realty... in the

MS. HAVILAND: [*Cont'd.*] interest of discretion...in the interest of taste...opted not to publish this particular address. So when you called, when you called with your *specific* request...

DR. SIMIAN: The...ah...front page, Ms. Haviland. That is how I knew. I realized...I *surmised*...the house would be for sale.

MS. HAVILAND: Did you?

DR. SIMIAN: And your firm...your size, your reputation...what other firm, I asked myself...

MS. HAVILAND: Well. What other firm *in this area*...

DR. SIMIAN: Surely I am not alone. You must admit, public preoccupation with...*this house*...I am not the first prospective buyer whose interest was initially piqued by reports of an altogether different nature....

MS. HAVILAND: No. You're not. *You most certainly are not.*

[*A tense pause.*]

Where have you been living?

DR. SIMIAN: Glen Ridge.

MS. HAVILAND: I'm not familiar with Glen Ridge.

DR. SIMIAN: No?

MS. HAVILAND: I have never even heard of Glen Ridge.

DR. SIMIAN: Beyond Ridge Falls. Near Beacon Ridge. Before Ridge Dale.

MS. HAVILAND: Suddenly you've decided to move?

DR. SIMIAN: Yes.

MS. HAVILAND: More room? Better schools? A sound investment strategy?

DR. SIMIAN: It's *time*.

MS. HAVILAND: Why *now*?

DR. SIMIAN: I've weathered a change in status.

MS. HAVILAND: Marital? Professional?

DR. SIMIAN: Both.

MS. HAVILAND: I hope it works out. For the best.

DR. SIMIAN: I hope.

[*Another stilted pause.*]

MS. HAVILAND: I'd like to point out some of the exterior features of the house, if I may. It's a Colonial, of course. The portico dates back to the Revolutionary War. Wildwood Park's own *Monticello.* Of course, the drainage system, the storm windows, the pool, the car port—-that's all contemporary.

DR. SIMIAN: Conservative, isn't it?

MS. HAVILAND: Classic. Beyond faddish. A constant. [MS. HAVILAND *points.*]

MS. HAVILAND: Notice the weathercock.

DR. SIMIAN: Where? I don't see...I can't quite...

MS. HAVILAND: The rooster.

DR. SIMIAN: The glare ...

MS. HAVILAND: The *silhouette.*

DR. SIMIAN: The sun's so *white* ...

MS. HAVILAND: Left of the chimney.

[DR. SIMIAN *uses his hands like a visor, shielding his eyes. He spots the weather vane.*]

DR. SIMIAN: Ah! Yes!

MS. HAVILAND: It wasn't bought; it was commissioned.

DR. SIMIAN: Impressive.

MS. HAVILAND: This house belongs on the dollar bill.

[*Another pause.*]

What sort of work do you do?

DR. SIMIAN: Medical.

MS. HAVILAND: You're not a journalist?

DR. SIMIAN: Should I be?

[MS. HAVILAND *glances from left to right. She speaks in a low, confidential tone.*]

MS. HAVILAND: I have to ask . . .

DR. SIMIAN: Yes?

MS. HAVILAND: You're not *undercover*, are you?

DR. SIMIAN: Under what?

MS. HAVILAND: You're not *wearing a wire*?

DR. SIMIAN: Excuse me?

MS. HAVILAND: You are not an *opportunist*, are you?

DR. SIMIAN: I rather expected I'd be asking the questions this afternoon.

MS. HAVILAND: I've learned the hard way, Dr. Simian. I can't be too careful. A few weeks ago, a man came, requesting to see the house. He brought a camcorder. He told me that his wife was back home, in Terre Haute, and that he intended to mail the tape back to her, before deciding. Well. You can imagine my surprise, when a few days later, I turned on the television, one of those alarmist news programs, and there it was. Edited. With an ominous soundtrack.

DR. SIMIAN: He'd sold the tape?

MS. HAVILAND: So forgive me if I exert caution.

DR. SIMIAN: My sole interest, Ms. Haviland, is in purchasing a home.

MS. HAVILAND: Thank goodness.

DR. SIMIAN: I am far more invested in a firm foundation, a basement which does not leak, a patio for summer parties than I am in . . . the unsavory.

MS. HAVILAND: Count yourself among a rarefied few.

DR. SIMIAN: If you distrust my *sincerity* . . .

MS. HAVILAND: I didn't say that.

DR. SIMIAN: I am *eager* to relocate. I have an *approved loan*. My intentions could not be more *serious*.

MS. HAVILAND: I am *relieved.*

DR. SIMIAN: Would you care to see my correspondence with the bank? A copy of my current mortgage?

MS. HAVILAND: Please. I—

DR. SIMIAN: Proof positive. The listing for my own home in *The Town Tattler.*

MS. HAVILAND: That isn't necessary. [DR. SIMIAN *pulls a folded newspaper from his inner breast pocket.*]

DR. SIMIAN: [*Reading.*] "Glen Ridge Charmer: Raised ranch, designed with family in mind. Three bedroom, two and a half bath, breakfast nook with skylight, basement rec room—"

MS. HAVILAND: I *apologize.*

[DR. SIMIAN *slaps the paper against his hand twice, to flatten it. He re-folds it, and returns it to his pocket. Another short pause.*]

DR. SIMIAN: I would be less than honest—

MS. HAVILAND: [*Quickly.*] Yes?

DR. SIMIAN: — if I didn't confess to an ulterior motive.

MS. HAVILAND: I suspected as much.

DR. SIMIAN: The reason I chose this house ... this *particular* house ... with its rather ... notorious ... history ...

MS. HAVILAND: Mm-hm?

DR. SIMIAN: I am ... I am ... I am a *bargain hunter.*

MS. HAVILAND: Oh. Well.

DR. SIMIAN: Correct me if I'm wrong, but I would assume, by-and-large, your average buyer would have, well ... *trepidation.* A fear that the house had somehow been ... *besmirched.* That it had absorbed its own history, and that it had somehow become ... *a hard sell.* But I am not a superstitious person. Karma, aura. These things mean nothing to me.

MS. HAVILAND: [*With significance.*] I have an unhappy surprise for you, Doctor.

[MS. HAVILAND *makes a thumbs-up gesture, which suggests that the asking price has soared.*]

DR. SIMIAN: No.

MS. HAVILAND: [*Nodding.*] *Oh yes.*

DR. SIMIAN: That's shocking.

MS. HAVILAND: Through the roof.

DR. SIMIAN: Is that the culture? The culture-at-large? Is that what we've become?

MS. HAVILAND: [*As a vulture.*] "Caaw! Caaw!"

DR. SIMIAN: You'll make me a cynical man, Ms. Haviland.

MS. HAVILAND: 1120 Sycamore Avenue has made me a cynical woman.

DR. SIMIAN: And the property values. In the neighborhood. They are—

MS. HAVILAND: Holding their own.

DR. SIMIAN: My, my.

MS. HAVILAND: Wildwood Park has not changed. It is the same enclave it always was. The traffic, of course, is heavier.

DR. SIMIAN: People ignore the blockades.

MS. HAVILAND: It's a constant battle.

DR. SIMIAN: License plates from Iowa. From California.

MS. HAVILAND: The furor will die down. By the time you're ready to take occupancy . . . should you decide to pursue the house . . . the traffic will taper, I assure you . . .

DR. SIMIAN: Naturally.

MS. HAVILAND: We still boast excellent schools. And I don't have to tell you, Doctor, the shopping in our little town is world-class. We have our own library. Our own post office. Our own women's auxiliary, and our own police force.

DR. SIMIAN: I couldn't help noticing. At the curb. The squad car.

MS. HAVILAND: A precaution against vandalism. A few weeks ago—a rock, some spray paint. *Eggs.*

DR. SIMIAN: I see.

MS. HAVILAND: An isolated incident.

DR. SIMIAN: It's to be expected.

MS. HAVILAND: It gives me great civic pride, Dr. Simian, to tell you that—for weeks—the front porch was teeming with candles. Bouquets. My own daughter made a wreath from sapling twigs. I was moved.

[*A pause.*]

Shall we go inside?

DR. SIMIAN: Please.

[MS. HAVILAND *begins the complicated process of opening the door.*]

MS. HAVILAND: You'll notice there are two double-bolt locks, with pick proof cylinders. In addition, the house has a twenty-four hour, fully computerized security system with built-in alarm, automatic police and fire notification, and an electronic fence. Oh, and the lights. They're on timers.

DR. SIMIAN: These precautions. They are . . . recent?

MS. HAVILAND: Yes. They are *new.* They were not here *before.*
[*Another brief pause.*]

Shall we?

[*They "enter" the house.*]

[*As* MS. HAVILAND *and* DR. SIMIAN *move from room to room throughout the house, they follow the markings on the blueprint beneath them. It's as though they are tokens on a board game, moving through implied three-dimensional space.*]

MS. HAVILAND: Eight thousand square feet, Doctor. Five bedrooms, four and a half baths.

[MS. HAVILAND *makes an extravagant gesture, indicating the vast expanse of the front hall.*]

Notice the upward sweep of the foyer. The walls rise the

MS. HAVILAND: full height of the house. The candelabra; that's brass. And look at the sunlight streaming down. We're flooded, aren't we? We're drowning in light.

[MS. HAVILAND *removes her sunglasses.*]

Dr. Simian. Your glasses. The color scheme.

DR. SIMIAN: Safe now, isn't it?

[DR. SIMIAN *removes his glasses, and slips them into his breast pocket.*]

Well, well. Isn't that strange. A cryptogram of some sort, isn't it?

MS. HAVILAND: Where?

DR. SIMIAN: Above the arch.

MS. HAVILAND: Ah, yes. *That.* It's Pennsylvania Dutch. A touch of *whimsy.*

DR. SIMIAN: What is it?

MS. HAVILAND: *Oh, dear.*

DR. SIMIAN: You're blushing.

MS. HAVILAND: It's a hex sign. *That is a hex sign.*

DR. SIMIAN: No.

MS. HAVILAND: For *good* luck.

DR. SIMIAN: One can't help thinking—-

MS. HAVILAND: Please. Don't.

[DR. SIMIAN *wanders ahead.*]

DR. SIMIAN: Is this the living room?

MS. HAVILAND: I must ask you, *don't barrel through.*

DR. SIMIAN: Forgive me.

MS. HAVILAND: I am conducting the tour.

DR. SIMIAN: Of course.

MS. HAVILAND: "Follow the Leader." *Indulge me.* Watch your step.

DR. SIMIAN: Thank you.

[*They "enter" the living room.*]

MS. HAVILAND: An exquisite space, Doctor. Floor-length windows. On the ceiling, rosettes. And the fireplace. You'll note its size. Its grandeur. Quarried marble. Venetian, I think.

[DR. SIMIAN *runs his hand along the mantel piece.*]

DR. SIMIAN: A substantial mantel.

MS. HAVILAND: Yes.

DR. SIMIAN: Can it support sculpture? Can it support *objets d' art?*

MS. HAVILAND: [*Curtly:*] I think you can *gauge*, Doctor.

DR. SIMIAN: The house is still furnished.

MS. HAVILAND: Not for long.

DR. SIMIAN: It looks...*inhabited.*

MS. HAVILAND: Things happened so quickly. The house was placed on the market so soon.

DR. SIMIAN: This room reminds me, Ms. Haviland, of an exhibit in a museum. The stillness. Its past hanging heavy in the air, unspoken.

MS. HAVILAND: There was of course, a will, provisions were naturally made, but in the absence of any...*beneficiaries*...the furniture will be sold at auction.

DR. SIMIAN: Aha.

MS. HAVILAND: The proceeds will benefit the Children's Legal Defense Fund.

DR. SIMIAN: An appropriate gesture.

MS. HAVILAND: If...*when* it is recovered...after its release from evidence...the Nubian statuette is expected to fetch a startling sum.

DR. SIMIAN: Surprise, surprise.

MS. HAVILAND: "Who," I ask myself. "Who would buy—"

DR. SIMIAN: Our society is predatory.

MS. HAVILAND: I'd almost bid on it myself. So I could take it home.

MS. HAVILAND: [*Cont'd.*] So I could take it home with me, and with my husband's hammer—

DR. SIMIAN: Yes.

MS. HAVILAND: I'd pay a hefty sum, just for the pleasure of seeing it *destroyed.*

DR. SIMIAN: Do you know, Ms. Haviland, the totems of our time?

MS. HAVILAND: The "totems?"

DR. SIMIAN: In Milwaukee, a stock pot on the stove. In Beverly Hills, an errant glove.

MS. HAVILAND: And among them....

DR. SIMIAN: ...yes...

MS. HAVILAND: ...in Wildwood Park...

DR. SIMIAN: ...exactly...

MS. HAVILAND: A Nubian statuette.

[*They "enter" the dining room.*]

You'll notice how the living room segues into the dining room. Dignified, isn't it? Vintage. You can comfortably seat up to twenty-four. Those sconces are from a tavern in the Hudson River Valley, circa 1890. You'd never guess...

[MS. HAVILAND *toys with a light switch.*]

...they're on a dimmer.

DR. SIMIAN: The kitchen can't be far behind.

MS. HAVILAND: Careful; that door swings.

[*They "enter" the kitchen.*]

A rustic look, but with every modern convenience. An electric oven, an industrial range, a microwave, and—for "old world" effect, a touch of antique romance—a wood-burning stove. Charming, yes? The cabinets are cherry wood, and the counter tops are Mexican tile. And you'll note, there's an island...cherry, too, with a granite top, pull-out shelves below, and of course...a...you see it, there...with a...a...*oh, dear...*

DR. SIMIAN: A what?

MS. HAVILAND: *A block.*

DR. SIMIAN: A block?

MS. HAVILAND: A *butcher* block.

[MS. HAVILAND *smiles a guilty smile.*]

DR. SIMIAN: Why, Ms. Haviland.

MS. HAVILAND: I'm horrible.

DR. SIMIAN: You've made a pun.

MS. HAVILAND: I'm a monster.

DR. SIMIAN: A pun, that's all.

MS. HAVILAND: I should have my tongue *cut out.*

[MS. HAVILAND *suppresses a giggle.*]

Oh, there. I've done it again.

DR. SIMIAN: You're giddy.

MS. HAVILAND: Shame on me. Shame on us both.

DR. SIMIAN: Humor, Ms. Haviland, fortifies.

[MS. HAVILAND *wipes tears from her eyes, composing herself.*]

MS. HAVILAND: This house, all day, every day. Dodging past the news vans. Those rapacious tourists. I fight my way past. *I have business here.* If it's made me loopy, Doctor, then I have every right to be.

DR. SIMIAN: Bravo.

MS. HAVILAND: My husband says it's nerves. My husband says all those infernal shutter-bugs, all those flash-bulbs, they've *seared* my *brain.*

DR. SIMIAN: A fanciful thought, Ms. Haviland.

MS. HAVILAND: My husband tells me that I take things to *heart.* That I should go on *automatic.* That is easy, Doctor, for *my* husband to say. It is, after all, his *forte.*

[MS. HAVILAND *snorts a laugh, a little bark, which afterwards makes her cheeks burn red.*]

DR. SIMIAN: I'd like to see the master bedroom.

MS. HAVILAND: [*Sadly.*] I'm exhausted. Frayed. That's the truth.

DR. SIMIAN: The bedroom, please.

MS. HAVILAND: But you haven't seen the den. You haven't seen the home office, the play room, the maid's suite—

[DR. SIMIAN *leaves the kitchen.* MS. HAVILAND *follows, suddenly strident.*]

MS. HAVILAND: *Don't charge ahead!*

DR. SIMIAN: I'm overeager.

MS. HAVILAND: I can't have people *wander.* I can't have people *traipsing through.*

DR. SIMIAN: I might go nosing in the linen cupboards.

MS. HAVILAND: Don't be absurd; it's not that.

DR. SIMIAN: I might empty the medicine chest.

MS. HAVILAND: *It's not that at all.*

DR. SIMIAN: I might pirate away knick-knacks, and open a souvenir stand on the corner.

MS. HAVILAND: I am responsible for the house, and its contents. I have *police* on my back. There are *attorneys.* A *battalion* of *lawyers.* Under the circumstances, it is an *overwhelming* duty.

DR. SIMIAN: I was insensitive.

MS. HAVILAND: My psychiatrist is *worried.* She *fears* for my *safety.* I am on *tranquilizers.*

DR. SIMIAN: It must be a strain.

[*They "enter" the master bedroom.*]

MS. HAVILAND: There are ceiling fans in all the bedrooms. You'll find that saves a fortune in cooling costs during the summer. A walk-in closet, which I dare say is larger than my living room.

DR. SIMIAN: Poignant, isn't it?

MS. HAVILAND: What?

DR. SIMIAN: There. On the floor, by the bed.

[*DR. SIMIAN points:*]

Empty shoes.

[*A palpable chill descends in the room.*]

This is where it began, yes?

MS. HAVILAND: [*Alarmed.*] *I beg your pardon?*

[*The following dialogue is rapid-fire, accelerating in speed, a crescendo.*]

DR. SIMIAN: The balcony doors.

MS. HAVILAND: I'd rather not.

DR. SIMIAN: They were left ajar? They were pried open?

MS. HAVILAND: You know I don't *approve* . . . I don't *appreciate* . . .

DR. SIMIAN: Around the lock, scuffs. Gouges.

MS. HAVILAND: I'm here to show the house. I'm not a *detective.* I am not a *talk show host.*

DR. SIMIAN: Forgive me. But I couldn't help noticing—-there—on the wainscoting—

MS. HAVILAND: The paint has been retouched.

DR. SIMIAN: Along the molding—

MS. HAVILAND: The carpets have all been shampooed.

DR. SIMIAN: Traces exist.

MS. HAVILAND: No. Where?

DR. SIMIAN: Splotches.

MS. HAVILAND: *There is nothing to notice.*

DR. SIMIAN: There. On the edge. Rimming the baseboards . . .

MS. HAVILAND: *I don't see a thing.*

DR. SIMIAN: The electrical outlets. Where are they?

MS. HAVILAND: [*Frightened.*] *What?*

DR. SIMIAN: It's a fair question.

MS. HAVILAND: It's a *taunt.* It's a *jibe.*

DR. SIMIAN: For *lamps*. For *clock-radios*. A *laptop*. These things require *voltage*.

MS. HAVILAND: All sorts of *appliances* require voltage, Dr. Simian. ALL SORTS.

DR. SIMIAN: A heating pad, perhaps! An electric blanket! Nothing menacing, nothing *pneumatic*.

MS. HAVILAND: Don't be *facetious*, Doctor.

DR. SIMIAN: SHOW ME.

MS. HAVILAND: Please!

DR. SIMIAN: *WHERE?*

MS. HAVILAND: Behind the headboard. And there. Under the vanity.

[*A short rest.* DR. SIMIAN *goes to the vanity table. He gets down on his hands and knees, and looks beneath it.*]

DR. SIMIAN: The wall plate. It's scorched.

MS. HAVILAND: What did you expect? It was *overburdened*, it was profoundly misused.

DR. SIMIAN: Hidden down here. Out of sight, out of mind?

MS. HAVILAND: There are still a few details . . .

DR. SIMIAN: A few *vestiges?*

MS. HAVILAND: A few REPAIRS.

[DR. SIMIAN *stands up. He looks in the mirror of the vanity, back at* MS. HAVILAND*'s reflection.*]

DR. SIMIAN: She was a singer for a while, wasn't she? She was on television in New York.

MS. HAVILAND: Dr. Simian, if you have inquiries about the house, about its *architecture*, its *design*, its *upkeep*—

DR. SIMIAN: She sold thigh cream, and overcame personal problems. And he made a fortune in junk bonds.

MS. HAVILAND: I'm sure I don't know.

DR. SIMIAN: Of course you know. *Everybody knows.*

MS. HAVILAND: I'm not *interested*.

DR. SIMIAN: You can't flip on the radio, you can't watch the news—

MS. HAVILAND: I *mute*, Doctor.

DR. SIMIAN: Even pick up a paper—

MS. HAVILAND: Because of my *professional obligations* ... my *necessary involvement* ... there are certain things I'd rather *not* know ...

[DR. SIMIAN *notices something on the wall. He points:*]

DR. SIMIAN: The little one. The youngest. The girl.

MS. HAVILAND: I have recommended to my employer that we re-move these photographs. They're unnerving. Prospective buy-ers are unhinged.

[DR. SIMIAN *traces the shape of the frame on the wall, with his fin-ger.*]

DR. SIMIAN: Freckles. A gap tooth.

MS. HAVILAND: Their eyes follow you. No matter where you turn.

DR. SIMIAN: What was her name?

MS. HAVILAND: All day, every day, they stare me down. Here at work. In *this* room. Outside, too. In line at the grocery store, the tabloids. On *T-shirts*, for God's sake, they've even been silk-screened ...

[DR. SIMIAN *notices another picture, this one on the night stand. He approaches it, and picks it up.*]

DR. SIMIAN: Here she is again, in a pageant of some kind.

MS. HAVILAND: *Put that down!*

DR. SIMIAN: Look at her. She's dressed as a radish. She's singing.

MS. HAVILAND: *You're not supposed to touch things!*

DR. SIMIAN: Oh, and look. Washing the family dog.

[DR. SIMIAN *puts the picture back in its place.*]

Is it true? *Even the dog?*

MS. HAVILAND: *You are disturbing things ... me ...*

DR. SIMIAN: The police posit that, sometime after three, she ... the

DR. SIMIAN: [Cont'd.] girl... heard a sound. If only she'd opted to hide under the bed, they said, if only she'd run out the back door, they said, if only her little legs—

[MS. HAVILAND *relents, and cuts him off.*]

MS. HAVILAND: *Heather.*

[*A pause.*]

Her name was Heather.

DR. SIMIAN: Take me to the nursery.

[*Another pause.*]

MS. HAVILAND: Do you have *children*, Dr. Simian?

DR. SIMIAN: More questions, Ms. Haviland?

MS. HAVILAND: Because if you don't have children... if you don't have *young* children... then the nursery is *irrelevant.*

DR. SIMIAN: Surely you are not offering the house on a room-by-room basis.

MS. HAVILAND: Don't insult me, Doctor.

DR. SIMIAN: I am interested in the entire structure. Not a portion thereof.

MS. HAVILAND: It's just, you've hardly inspected the house. The living room, the kitchen, the dining room, and nary a remark. "He's bound to have questions about the plumbing," I say to myself, "and radon, and chimney flues. He'll want to know about the new roof, about winter insulation." *But no!*

DR. SIMIAN: Ms. Haviland, I—

MS. HAVILAND: *Oh, no!* With you it's all... hex signs... and hollow shoes... and *little girls.*

DR. SIMIAN: There are still whole rooms—

MS. HAVILAND: The tour is over.

DR. SIMIAN: *Entire wings—*

MS. HAVILAND: It's half-past-five.

DR. SIMIAN: The backyard. The guest house.

MS. HAVILAND: The work day has come to a close.

DR. SIMIAN: I've driven a great distance—

MS. HAVILAND: Please leave.

DR. SIMIAN: I can't readily arrange a second visit—

MS. HAVILAND: Wildwood Park is a private community. A discreet community. It is not some sordid *theme park*, Doctor. It is not a *freak show*, with its tent flaps spread—-no, *torn*—open for the nation's *amusement*. It is not some *dime store, penny-dreadful, Stephen King*—

DR. SIMIAN: A daughter, six, and a son, eight.

[*A pause.* MS. HAVILAND *blushes. Slowly and definitively—like a lawyer giving a summation of evidence—* DR. SIMIAN *continues.*]

DR. SIMIAN: [*Cont'd.*] My daughter's name is Sarah. She has a widow's peak, hazel eyes, and what at first might seem like an extra appendage but which, upon closer examination, reveals itself to be a very old, very odorous stuffed bear, a veteran of her bouts with the flu, the washing machine, and even a long, torturous night spent, abandoned, in the supermarket. He has one eye, and leaves an unmistakable trail of fleece wherever he goes. His name, should you require it for the record, is Mister Pete. My son is Joshua. Because he was slow to walk, he was misdiagnosed with cerebral palsy, and it gave us quite a scare. Now he is graceful and long of limb. He is obsessed with choo-choo trains. The court—at the recommendation of my wife's psychologist—has granted custody solely to me.

[*A long pause.* MS. HAVILAND *swallows, hard. Her face is pinched. Finally.*]

MS. HAVILAND: It's upstairs.

[*They climb in silence up a flight of stairs to the nursery.*]

The wallpaper is a pale green candy-stripe, suitable for a boy or girl. The border is Beatrix Potter. Window guards, of course. An intercom, so wherever you are in the house, you never feel far away. The children have their own bath. The basin is low, and the tub has a rail. As you can see, the

MS. HAVILAND: [*Cont'd.*] emphasis here ... the design insures ... *attempts* to insure ... a child's *safety.*

[MS. HAVILAND *sighs, heavily.*]

I want *desperately* to sell this house. I do not like being a *sentinel.* I do not like standing by quietly as people *gape* and *mock* and *jeer.* It's a disease, Doctor, and it is contagious, and some days, it's true, I fear *I am catching it.* This is not a *movie.* This is not *television.*

[MS. HAVILAND *cries, softly.*]

What I do is necessary. Houses are bought and sold. But sometimes ... what I do here feels like *desecration.* Walking in their tracks. Sifting through their things. *Oh, God, forgive me.*

DR. SIMIAN: Did you know the victims, Ms. Haviland?

MS. HAVILAND: No.

DR. SIMIAN: Even a passing acquaintance?

MS. HAVILAND: No.

DR. SIMIAN: Then permit me to suggest ... this unfortunate event wields far greater power over you than perhaps it should.

MS. HAVILAND: *It's all I think about.* I have my own husband, my own children, we're remodeling our place on the Eastern shore, my mother has *cancer*— these things, they are *the substance of my life* — and now they are merely *distractions* to keep me from *obsessing* ... to drive the endless litany of questions from my head. *Why that night? Why those children? The parents, were they spared the sight, were they taken first, or were they forced to witness ... And ... this, Doctor, haunts me the most ... what sort of man ... what kind of brute creature ...*

DR. SIMIAN: Anyone, I suppose, would wonder.

MS. HAVILAND: It's worse than *wondering.* Far more *extreme.*

[MS. HAVILAND *cannot continue. She musters strength, and then:*]

Once ... a canceled appointment ... I barricaded the front door ... reset the alarm .... drew the blinds ... from her closet, a robe, blue with pink piping ... and I sat in the study ...

MS. HAVILAND: [*Cont'd.*] swathed in her smell...poring through family albums. Birthdays. Christmases. The first day at school, afternoons at the Fair, anniversary notes, private, still perfumed ...They were not mine, but they *could've* been mine, they might as well have been mine...I am such a *hypocrite*, Doctor.

DR. SIMIAN: It's all right.

MS. HAVILAND: I sat, alone in this house, with the lights out, and I waited.

DR. SIMIAN: For what?

MS. HAVILAND: The balcony door to open. The soft, almost noise-less crunch of rubber soles on white shag...

DR. SIMIAN: Why?

MS. HAVILAND: *If God gave me the chance to see evil, Doctor, then I would look. And that's a terrible thing to know about oneself.*

[MS. HAVILAND *looks at* DR. SIMIAN, *pleadingly. He responds in a tender voice.*]

DR. SIMIAN: You are...

MS. HAVILAND: Go ahead. Say it.

DR. SIMIAN: You are a *very bad* little monkey.

MS. HAVILAND: I want my own life *back*. My own *concerns*.

[DR. SIMIAN *takes her hand.* MS. HAVILAND *takes a moment to calm herself.*]

MR. SIMIAN: Take a breath. We don't have to move. Remember, Ms. Haviland, that you have your *own* home. Your *own* retreat.

MS. HAVILAND: A new family. Here. That would be nice. An *antidote*, yes, Doctor? Isn't that the word? I hope that you will contemplate this house. I hope that with all my heart.

DR. SIMIAN: I intend to.

MS. HAVILAND: I would like...I would like to be free of this. And I would like you...

DR. SIMIAN: Yes?

MS. HAVILAND: You...and your children...a fresh start.

DR. SIMIAN: Remember, Ms. Haviland that you have your *own* home. Your own *retreat.*

MS. HAVILAND: [*Consoled.*] Yes.

[DR. SIMIAN *slips his dark glasses out of his pocket. He puts them back on.*]

DR. SIMIAN: Would you see me to the porch?

MS. HAVILAND: My pleasure, Doctor.

[*Again, they back-track in silence, this time without any obvious tension. They leave the house, and step outside onto the porch.*]

I'm embarrassed. My employer.

DR. SIMIAN: The robe, the snapshots.

MS. HAVILAND: If they knew . . .

DR. SIMIAN: Not a word.

MS. HAVILAND: Here's my card. If you have any questions, don't hesitate.

DR. SIMIAN: [*Taking the card:*] I won't.

MS. HAVILAND: I'm sorry. My *display.*

DR. SIMIAN: Don't mention it.

MS. HAVILAND: I've shown you quite an afternoon, haven't I?

DR. SIMIAN: Quite.

MS. HAVILAND: You. A stranger.

DR. SIMIAN: I did wonder——

MS. HAVILAND: Yes?

DR. SIMIAN: A musing. A curiosity. Nothing pragmatic. Nothing "nuts and bolts."

MS. HAVILAND: Please.

DR. SIMIAN: One thing concerns me.

MS. HAVILAND: Oh?

DR. SIMIAN: No arrest. No conviction.

MS. HAVILAND: Sadly enough.

DR. SIMIAN: No substantive leads.

MS. HAVILAND: Every day, we pray.

DR. SIMIAN: As you suggest . . . there exists the possibility of . . . well, the perpetrator . . . he might return.

MS. HAVILAND: I see my paranoia has spread.

DR. SIMIAN: No, no. Your *prescience*. It's often been documented. Many a criminal—in spite of the immense risk—will return to the scene of the crime.

MS. HAVILAND: I can't *imagine* . . .

DR. SIMIAN: Regardless of the alarms. The reversible bolts. The electronic fences. Even the squad car at the curb.

MS. HAVILAND: But why?

DR. SIMIAN: All in pursuit of the covert thrill that comes with the successful commission of a wrongful act.

MS. HAVILAND: Is that *true*? Is that what they *say*?

DR. SIMIAN: It would not shock me to learn, Ms. Haviland, that you yourself had escorted the culprit through these halls.

MS. HAVILAND: It is a good thing that I am so thorough, Doctor. So vigilant.

DR. SIMIAN: He feigns interest in the housing market. Comes well-armed, perhaps, with the classifieds. You interrogate him, and for every question, he has a ready quip. He is from an obscure town. He is a banker. No. A lawyer. No. A doctor.

[MS. HAVILAND *freezes. Her whole body seems to clench.* DR. SIMIAN *takes a step closer to her.*]

MS. HAVILAND: Yes.

[DR. SIMIAN *takes another step, even closer.*]

DR. SIMIAN: He is newly married. No. Expecting a baby.

MS. HAVILAND: No. Separated.

[*And another step closer.*]

DR. SIMIAN: He has grown daughters. No. Adopted sons. No—

[DR. SIMIAN *is so near, she can feel his breath.*]

MS. HAVILAND: *A boy and a girl. One of each. She has a toy ... it's plush ... Mister Somebody....*

[DR. SIMIAN *cocks an eyebrow, and waits for* MS. HAVILAND *to finish.*]

I can't....I don't.....oh, God....

[DR. SIMIAN *reaches down, and takes her hand. He separates her fingers with his own, and intertwines them. He speaks in a sensuous, hypnotic tone.*]

[*Deep within* MS. HAVILAND, *continental plates begin to shift.*]

DR. SIMIAN: You usher him over the threshold. As you patter on— stucco and mini-blinds and Formica and chintz—with each step he's reliving, with a kind of salacious glee, the very night he thwarted every fragile notion of civilized behavior. The very night he let loose the constraints of his own base nature, and made the very darkest kind of history.

[*With his free hand, gently,* DR. SIMIAN *takes* MS. HAVILAND *by the chin. He raises her face to meet his.*]

[*They stare at one another.*]

Tell me. *Do you ever consider that possibility?*

MS. HAVILAND: No. I do not.

DR. SIMIAN: Perhaps you should.

MS. HAVILAND: *I emphatically do not.* I can't... *afford* ... to entertain such ... *notions.* It would render my job untenable.

DR. SIMIAN: Yes.

MS. HAVILAND: It would induce paralysis. It would hold me captive.

DR. SIMIAN: Precisely.

MS. HAVILAND: *I cannot live my life that way.*

DR. SIMIAN: You're a wise woman.

[MS. HAVILAND *speaks with a very slight, almost imperceptible tremor.*]

MS. HAVILAND: I hope that you will consider this house. I hope that you are in the market, and I hope that you will buy.

[DR. SIMIAN *nods in the direction of the squad car.*]

DR. SIMIAN: Perhaps, when I leave, you'll offer the policeman a cup of coffee.

MS. HAVILAND: No.

DR. SIMIAN: Perhaps you'll have a conversation.

MS. HAVILAND: We've never met. I see him every morning, but we've never met.

DR. SIMIAN: Perhaps today is the day.

MS. HAVILAND: I do not know him.

DR. SIMIAN: That doesn't preclude a polite introduction.

MS. HAVILAND: I know *you*, Doctor.

DR. SIMIAN: Thank you.

MS. HAVILAND: You are the man whom I know.

DR. SIMIAN: Thank you *so much.*

[DR. SIMIAN *lets her hand go. He takes a step back.*]

[MS. HAVILAND *wavers, starts to melt into him. She holds herself back.*]

It's been a lovely afternoon. And the house. The house is beautiful.

[DR. SIMIAN *turns to leave.* MS. HAVILAND *calls him back.*]

MS. HAVILAND: You're interested, then?

DR. SIMIAN: Yes.

[*Again*, DR. SIMIAN *turns to go. Again,* MS. HAVILAND *stops him.*]

MS. HAVILAND: [*Impulsively.*] Dr. Simian?

DR. SIMIAN: Ms. Haviland?

MS. HAVILAND: [*Darkly; almost seductively.*] You *are* interested?

[DR. SIMIAN *smiles an enigmatic smile. He holds up* MS. HAVI-

LAND's *business card. With deliberate slowness, he slips it into his breast pocket. He pats his heart, three times.*]

[*They stare at one another a long time. Finally,* DR. SIMIAN *leaves.*]

[MS. HAVILAND *lingers after him for a moment. Slowly, she turns back, to gaze at the house.*]

[*Slow fade.*]

END OF PLAY

The Scarlet Letter
by Nathaniel Hawthorne
Adapted for the stage by
James F. DeMaiolo

Leslie Fiedler pronounced it the first American tragedy. F.O. Mathiessen considered it the "Puritan Faust." Richard B. Sewall compared its inexorable dramatic force to King Lear. These chieftains of American literature were not, as one might suspect referring to a play by O'Neill. They are not in fact, referring to a play at all, but to a masterpiece of nineteenth century fiction. Until now, it appeared that Nathaniel Hawthorne's haunting drama of judgment, alienation and redemption would be forever confined to the page. The Scarlet Letter continues to be the most frequently read novel in American high schools today as well as one of the most widely circulated novels in the American library system. And now comes the stage version to do it justice.

A century and a half after its first incarnation, James DeMaiolo has forged an alliance of craft and spirit so potent in its own right and so faithful to Hawthorne's original that his stage version is certain to compel all non-believers to recant and take heed. The audience joins the chorus as they weigh the American contract of freedom against the fine print of convention and taboo.

Paper•ISBN 1-55783-243-9 • $6.95
Performance rights available from APPLAUSE

APPLAUSE

GHOST IN THE MACHINE

A New Play
by David Gilman

"A devilishly clever puzzler of a comedy...it traps us in a web of uncertainty till we begin to wecond guess with the characters."

—Jan Stewart, *New York Newsday*

"A vastly entertaining whodunit, a chess game with human pieces that does not limit itself...Gilman teases us with philosophical questions on the nature of reality..."

—Laurie Winer, *The Los Angeles Times*

"Atight theatrical puzzle, the play echoes both the menacing personal relationships at the center of Harold Pinter's work and the complex mathematical equations that animate Tom Stoppard...but it is also very much of its own thing."

—Hedy Weiss, *The Chicago Sun Times*

Ghost in the the Machine begins with a common situation-that of a missing fifty dollar bill-and spins it into intriguing questions of probability, chance and the complexities of musical composition: illusion and reality.

Paper•ISBN 1-55783-228-5• $6.95
Performance rights available from APPLAUSE

APPLAUSE

BEST AMERICAN SHORT PLAYS 1991-1992

Edited by Howard Stein and Glenn Young

The Best American Short Play series includes a careful mixture of offerings from many prominent established playwrights, as well as up and coming younger playwrights. This collection of short plays truly celebrates the economy and style of the short play form. Doubtless, a must for any library!

Making Contact by **PATRICIA BOSWORTH** • Dreams of Home by **MIGDALIA CRUZ** • A Way with Words by **FRANK D. GILROY** • Prelude and Liebestod by **TERRENCE MCNALLY** • Success by **ARTHUR KOPIT** • The Devil and Billy Markham by **SHEL SILVERSTEIN** • The Last Yankee by **ARTHUR MILLER** • Snails by **SUZAN-LORI PARKS** • Extensions by **MURRAY SCHISGAL** • Tone Clusters by **JOYCE CAROL OATES** • You Can't Trust the Male by **RANDY NOOJIN** • Struck Dumb by **JEAN-CLAUDE VAN ITALLIE** and **JOSEPH CHAIKIN** • The Open Meeting by **A.R.GURNEY**

$12.95 • PAPER • ISBN: 1-55783-113-0 $25.95 • CLOTH• ISBN: 1-55783-112-2

BEST AMERICAN SHORT PLAYS 1990

Salaam, Huey Newton, Salaam by **ED BULLINS** • Naomi in the Living Room by **CHRISTOPHER DURANG** • The Man Who Climbed the Pecan Trees by **HORTON FOOTE** • Teeth by **TINA HOWE** • Sure Ting by **DAVID IVES** • Christmas Eve on Orchard Street by **ALLAN KNEE** • Akhmatova by **ROMULUS LINNEY** • Unprogrammed by **CAROL MACK** • The Cherry Orchard by **RICHARD NELSON** • Hidden in this Picture by **AARON SORKIN** • Boy Meets Girl by **WENDY WASSERSTEIN** • Abstinence by **LANFORD WILSON**

$24.95 CLOTH ISBN 1-55783-084-3 • $12.95 PAPER ISBN 1-55783-085-1

APPLAUSE

BEST AMERICAN SHORT PLAYS 1993-1994

"THE WORK IS FIRST RATE! IT IS EXCITING TO FIND THIS COLLECTON OF TRULY SHORT PLAYS BY TRULY ACCOMPLISHED PLAYWRIGHTS...IDEAL FOR SCHOOL READING AND WORKSHOP PRODUCTIONS:...' —KLIATT

Window of Opportunity by JOHN AUGUSTINE • Barry, Betty, and Bill by RENÉE TAYLOR/JOSEPH BOLOGNA • Come Down Burning by KIA CORTHRON • For Whom the Southern Belle Tolls by CHRISTOPHER DURANG • The Universal Language by DAVID IVES • The Midlife Crisis of Dionysus by GARRISON KEILLOR • The Magenta Shift by CAROL K. MACK • My Left Breast by SUSAN MILLER • The Interview by JOYCE CAROL OATES • Tall Tales from The Kentucky Cycle by ROBERT SCHENKKAN • Blue Stars by STUART SPENCER • An Act of Devotion by DEBORAH TANNEN • Zipless by ERNEST THOMPSON • Date With A Stranger by CHERIE VOGELSTEIN

$15.95 • PAPER • ISBN: 1-55783-199-8 • $29.95 • CLOTH• ISBN: 1-55783-200-5

BEST AMERICAN SHORT PLAYS 1992-1993

Little Red Riding Hood by BILLY ARONSON • Dreamers by SHEL SILVERSTEIN • Jolly by DAVID MAMET • Show by VICTOR BUMBALO • A Couple With a Cat by TONY CONNOR • Bondage by DAVID HENRY HWANG • The Drowing of Manhattan by JOHN FORD NOONAN • The Tack Room by RALPH ARZOOMIAN • The Cowboy, the Indian, and the Fervent Feminist by MURRAY SCHISGAL • The Sausage Eaters by STEPHEN STAROSTA • Night Baseball by GABRIEL TISSIAN • It's Our Town, Too by SUSAN MILLER • Watermelon Rinds by REGINA TALYOR • Pitching to the Star by DONALD MARGULIES • The Valentine Fairy by ERNEST THOMPSON • Aryan Birth by ELIZABETH PAGE

$15.95 • Paper • ISBN 1-55783-166-1 • $29.95 • cloth • ISBN 1-55783-167-X

BEST AMERICAN SHORT PLAYS 1995-1996

Edited by Howard Stein and Glenn Young

Fitting Rooms by SUSAN CINOMAN • Scribe's Paradox or the Mechanical Rabbit by MICHAEL FEINGOLD • Home Section by JANUSZ GLOWACKI • Degas, C'est Moi by DAVID IVES • The St. Valentine's Day Massacre by ALLAN KNEE • Old Blues by JONATHAN LEVY • Dearborn Heights by CASSANDRA MEDLEY • American Dreamers by LAVONNE MUELLER • When It Comes Early by JOHN FORD NOONAN • The Original Last Wish Baby by WILLIAM SEEBRING • The Mystery School by PAUL SELIG • The Sandalwood Box by MAC WELLMAN •

$15.95 • PAPER • ISBN: 1-55783-255-2 • $29.95 • CLOTH• ISBN: 1-55783-254-4

BEST AMERICAN SHORT PLAYS 1994-1995

A Stye of the Eye by CHRISTOPHER DURANG • Buck Simple by CRAIG FOLS • Two Mens'es Daughter by J.E. FRANKLIN • An Interview by DAVID MAMET • WASP by STEVE MARTIN • Hot Line by ELAINE MAY • Life Support by MAX MITCHELL • The Whole Shebang by RICH ORLOFFF • Dear Kenneth Blake by JACQUELYN REINGOLD • The Cannibal Masque by RONALD RIBMAN • The Artist and the Model by MURRAY SCHISGAL • The Spelling of Coynes by JULES TASCA • The Wreck on the Five-Twenty-Five by THORNTON WILDER • Lot 13: The Bone Violin by DOUG WRIGHT

$15.95 • Paper • ISBN 1-55783-232-3 • $29.95 • cloth • ISBN 1-55783-231-5

APPLAUSE